K9 Officer's Manual

R. S. Eden

Detselig Enterprises Ltd.
Calgary, Alberta

Temeron Books Inc.
Bellingham, Washington

K9 Officer's Manual

© 1993 R.S. Eden

Canadian Cataloguing in Publication Data

Eden, R.S. (Robert S.)
  K9 Officer's Manual

  ISBN 1-55059-062-6 (Detselig : bound). -- ISBN 1-55059-061-8 (Detselig : pbk.). – ISBN 1-895510-04-X (Temeron : bound). – ISBN 1-895510-03-1 (Temeron : pbk.)

  1. Police–Handbooks, manuals, etc. 2. Police dogs–Handbooks, manuals, etc. I.Title.
HV8025.E32 1993   363.2   C93-091239-X

Detselig Enterprises Ltd.
210, 1220 Kensington Road NW
Calgary, Alberta T2N 3P5

Temeron Books Inc.
P.O. Box 896
Bellingham, Washington 98227

All rights reserved. No part of this book may be reproduced in any form or by any means without permission in writing from the publisher.

Printed in Canada   SAN 115-0324

Temeron ISBN 1-895510-04-X hb   Detselig ISBN 1-55059-062-6 hb
               1-895510-03-1 pb   1-55059-061-8 pb

Sgt. Larry Young

This book is dedicated to the memory of Sergeant Larry Young, who was shot and killed during an ERT operation when serving a warrant on a drug trafficker. A highly dedicated and respected police officer, Larry was a friend who taught me never to quit. If it hadn't been for his encouragement I would not be the officer I am today. I hope I can live up to his expectations.

Stella, this book is for you and the kids, so others may know of the special family left behind. You are not forgotten.

Contents

Preface

The Experts Say . . .

1. K9 Administration 3

2. Patrol Officer's Guide to K9 17

3. K9 Officers 33

4. The Basics of Survival 43

5. Range Training for K9 Applications 55

6. Handler Control vs. Reasonable Force 69

7. Tracking 79

8. Tracking On-line vs. Off-line 91

9	Officer Effectiveness on the Track	103
10	Building Searches	111
11	Flashlight Techniques	123
12	Vehicle Stops	133
13	Emergency Response Team Support	147
14	Chemical Agents	155
15	K9 Testimony	161
16	Police Dog Protection and Safety	167
17	K9 Trauma Care	175
18	Valor	193
	K9 Training and Usage Logs	209

List of Photo Subjects

Chapter 2

Proper backup officer position using one officer

Backup positions when two officers are available

Psychological difference between officer on track alone and with backup

Officer Kevin O'Shaugnessy and K9 Jake, who both received gunshot wounds when backup teams fell behind

Chapter 3

Commands to the K9 under panic situtations

Chapter 4

Deputy John McCroskey and K9 Ward, who died from stab wounds

Officer Bob Willey and K9 Cody, who captured the suspect who killed K9 Ward

Chapter 5

Shoot and move technique

Building search – improper positioning of the dog

Building search – proper positioning of the dog

Left-handed officer and dog trained on the right side

Chapter 7

Confronting suspect with dog

Positioning so suspect focuses on the dog, not on officer approach

Multiple backups and triangulation

Chapter 8

Technique for pursuing fleeing suspects

Reflective off-line tracking harness

Chapter 10
    Door entries into building searches

Chapter 11
    Backup light
    Flashlight position during suspect search
    Invitation to disaster – backlighting from backup officer
    Dangers of overuse of flashlight

Chapter 12
    Patrol car remote door release
    Deployment of K9 to check felony vehicle
    Deployment of K9 to extricate suspect from vehicle
    Potential dangers of car stops

Chapter 13
    Vancouver City Police Emergency Response Team working with K9 unit

Chapter 16
    K9 temperature monitoring system
    K9 body vest

Chapter 18
    Constable Michael Buday, RCMP
    Lt. Fred House, Utah State Department of Corrections
    Officer Harry B. (Jim) Hanson, Anchorage Police Department
    Officer Randy Gehrke and K9 Zach
    Deputy Tom Mitchum and K9 Lucky
    Officer Jim Weaver and K9 Kim

Preface

When I sat down at the keyboard to start the introduction to this book, I thought about many ideas I wanted to express. I didn't know how to get across the importance of this manual and the sincerity with which I wrote it. I want this book to help save the lives of the officers who read it.

I also want administrators and patrol officers to better understand the needs of the dog handler. It is important for administrators and patrol officers to understand the potential, as well as the limitations of dog teams. K9 handlers are in one of the highest risk positions in law enforcement, yet very few departments spend extra time and finances sending them on programs to teach them how to handle those increased risks.

I have known officers who have died needlessly at the hands of others. I also know many police officers whose dogs have been killed in the line of duty. In most cases where a dog is killed while actively pursuing a suspect, the officer's life is spared as a result.

There is no question as to the value of a properly maintained dog team. The risks are often high in respect to liability and personal safety. However the achievements realized in the protection of lives and property more than justify the risks. I hope this book gives all members of law enforcement a better understanding of K9 teams.

– R.S. Eden

Disclaimer

While every effort has been made to ensure that the methods and recommendations contained in this book are sound and accurate, the results of K9 police work vary with each K9 team and the unique circumstances of any particular incident. Neither the author nor the publisher accepts any legal or moral responsibility nor any liability for the outcome of any case or incident, nor for any errors or omissions.

Acknowledgements

My years as a dog handler have been a challenge, with as many heartaches as rewards. Although some of this manual is a result of my own experience, by far most of it is based on information other officers have taken the time to teach me.

Deputy Jack McDonald and Bruce Jackson, with their many hours of lectures, have been a large part of my makeup as a handler. Dave Boynton of the Bremerton Police Department, Jeff Fenton of Phoenix and Brian Amm of Calgary have all strongly influenced me as a trainer.

A special thanks must go to Tom Haworth, NCO in charge of the Surrey Detachment, RCMP Dog Services section. Tom has been a close friend for many years and his expertise as an instructor and dog handler is surpassed by none. Also thanks to Gord Ney, a friend who has constantly encouraged and aided me with my training programs for the last five years. Dr. David Huff, my department veterinarian, has likewise been an excellent resource with a wealth of knowledge.

Further thanks go to Garry Gilliam of the Anchorage Police Department. To Tom House, the House, Buday, and Hanson families, a special thanks for assisting me in researching the incidents involving their friends and family members who were K9 handlers killed in the line of duty. I will be eternally grateful to these families, for the information obtained and shared by them will help other officers to be more aware of the daily dangers they face. With this information, the memory of these officers lives within each of us who still work the streets and may ultimately save our lives.

My thanks to officers such as Mike Dean, Kevin O'Shaugnessy, Randy Gehrke, Stan Boyes, John McCroskey, Tom Mitchum and others, who have shared their experiences so we could benefit from them. I'm grateful to Bob Willey, Gord and Tracey McGuinness, M. Paul Cook, Lynn Hurren, Bill Clede, Terry Fleck, Peter Turton, and Darwin Drader, who went over the fine details with me to ensure the book had the desired qualities.

These are the people whom I have learned from. This book is simply a compilation of techniques acquired and knowledge gleaned through my experience.

To my wife Ruth-Anne and my four sons David, Bryan, Jared, and Matthew, a special thanks for the understanding and patience they have given me over the years – for the times I never seem to get home from shift on time and the days they never see me due to my work . . . and for the time lost with the family while writing this manuscript.

Of course I can't forget my K9 partner Lance, who has bailed me out of numerous situations and taught me about myself and my abilities as a handler.

The Experts Say . . .

When I reviewed Bob Eden's *Dog Training for Law Enforcement* (Detselig Press, 1985) I called it "the best, most practical and easiest to understand dog training book I've ever read." Bob's writing style is easy to read. His knowledge of the subject is extensive and exemplary. And when a book publisher asked me to write a manual for K9 officers, I readily recommended that Bob Eden be given the job. After reading *K9 Officer's Manual*, I'm glad I did.

Any failings of K9 units rest not only on the dog or on the K9 officer. The faults also lie with the failure of administrators to understand the special requirements of running a police service dog program, or the lack of understanding by other officers in how to work with the K9 unit.

You Need This Book . . .

- If you are a police administrator, you need this book.
- If you are a patrol officer, you should read this book.
- If you are a K9 officer, there is no other source that will provide you with as much information, help, and ammunition as this book.

I'm particularly impressed with how Bob Eden organized his work, with a section directed to administrators, another to patrol officers, and the largest part devoted to K9 officers themselves. Then he adds the true stories of heroic K9s and their handlers, for the lessons to be learned.

The benefits of having a K9 unit are undeniable, even though they are not all of epic proportion. When I was a patrol officer with the Windsor, Connecticut police department, with just 40 sworn then, we had a K9 team. Many times Officer Ed Banasiak and K9 Gobi were called in to handle situations we couldn't resolve amicably or efficiently. One of the lesser instances was a beer fest then held annually in town. When it came time to clear the crowd at closing time, the party was not always ready to stop. With Ed and Gobi on the point, the wedge of officers had no problem moving the mob off the premises.

Such situations don't make for dramatic reports or newspaper headlines, but they sure made my job easier. They avoided what could have become a nasty event. Was it worth the cost of maintaining a K9 unit? From my point of view, you bet your life it was. And it could have been a situation where the bet *was* my life. Too often, I see command decisions made on less than complete information. You owe it to yourself and your department to understand the unique circumstances of a K9 operation. I know of no better way to achieve that than by reading Bob Eden's *K9 Officer's Manual*.

Bill Clede
Windsor CT Police Dept., Ret.
Technical Editor,
Law and Order

Bob Eden's new book, *K9 Officer's Manual*, is something better than a mere manual. It is a supermarket of ideas for the conscientious K9 officer. Like any supermarket, you won't take the whole inventory every time you go to it. Instead, you will take what you need at the time and leave the rest on the shelves, ready to be used at some later date. Believe me when I say that if you stay in the K9 business for any length of time, you will have to face every issue Eden addresses.

There are passages with which you may disagree, and others with which you will heartily concur. However, there are none that have not been thoroughly and objectively covered. Constable Eden analyzes topics such as "Short vs Long Handler Schools," "Find and Bark vs Find and Bite" and "On-line vs Off-line Tracking." He details pros and cons of each side; leaving the reader to choose which approach is best in his or her own situation.

The book is liberally salted with accounts of K9 applications gone awry, and others successfully resolved. These accounts drive home Eden's key points about officer safety, scent, use of force and a host of other topics. Separate sections of the book are written for handlers, administrators and patrol officers. For people in any of those categories, *K9 Officer's Manual* is a much needed catalyst for thought. Every K9 handler needs to get this book.

```
Officer Steve White
Trainer
Seattle Police K9 Unit
```

This book is a "must read" for every K9 handler, K9 unit supervisor and administrator. Finally, a police K9 textbook has been written which covers everything from A to Z, including actual K9 deployment scenarios. I have read many books on police K9 training and application. This book is by far the most detailed and informative of its kind.

I have learned a great deal by reading this book. Bob Eden's knowledge in this field is commanding, to say the least. The information in the book is invaluable. A true reference manual that I will refer to time and time again.

```
P.O. John Andrews
K9 Handler
Chicago Police Department
```

1
K9
Administration

Introduction To Police Administrators

There are many differences in the way law enforcement agencies organize and operate their K9 units. Whatever those differences may be, there is one factor common to most departments. In the United States and Canada, budget constraints almost always hit the dog section of a department before any other section.

This has a direct effect on the officers within the section and their ability to perform successfully on the street, which in turn affects the safety of both the dog handlers and line officers they support.

Budget Constraints

Budget constraint is a necessary evil with any agency. Cutting costs in any section is difficult and there is never an easy solution. The difference between the dog section and other sections of the department is the liability factor. If you have dogs on the street, the department's potential for lawsuits will be considerable if those teams do not have the most up-to-date training available. Training budgets for a K9 section (including courses, in-service training and associated equipment) cannot afford to be conservative. To limit budgets will only put the program and department at risk.

Record Keeping

Any good police service dog needs to be worked consistently and regularly to keep him efficient in all areas of training. While it is preferable to have a full time-training program operating, budgets of small departments may not be capable of supporting a full- time in-service program. At the minimum, weekly in-service training programs are required to keep K9 teams proficient.

With liability concerns as they are today, any administrator who is responsible for a dog unit has to make training and record keeping a priority. This record keeping must document all weekly in-service training which is required to keep a team at a basic level of proficiency. Note that 35 to 40 percent of a K9 team's in-service time must be spent on training, in order for them to maintain a minimum standard of proficiency. This is considered a minimum. Agencies which fail to support their K9 teams with adequate training time are putting their officers at risk while also running a high risk of liability for their department.

Good record keeping cannot be stressed enough, and accurate training records are only the first in a series of documents that the dog unit should maintain. Whenever a team is deployed – regardless of success – submit a report outlining the application and circumstances of the event. Document any use of force by the dog on a suspect; if the dog has made physical contact with the suspect, the injury site should be photographed and held on file.

If adequately defined, these deployment records not only supply pertinent data for court purposes, but can also reveal patterns for the unit's head trainer. By studying a series of deployment reports over a given period of time, the training officer can determine weaknesses in a particular dog team's training. For example a team may exhibit a high rate of failure on tracking applications where there is a time delay in excess of ten minutes, or where the temperature is higher than 15.5 degrees Celsius (60 degrees Fahrenheit). This could be indicative of a dog that lacks stamina and needs work in these areas.

Health records on each dog are vital to ensure the dog's shots and medical checkups are kept up to date. This protects the department as well.

Record keeping can often be a cumbersome task, as any police officer knows. However it is the best protection you have against liabilities. It can be a double-edged sword as well, as any documentation can be subpoenaed by defense counsel or litigation attorneys. It is prudent for officers to write their reports with this in mind.

K9 Training Schools

Abbreviated Training Schools

A common arrangement used by administrators in the United States in attempts to cut costs is to send officers on abbreviated training programs. They reason they cannot afford to send the officer away on a twelve- to sixteen-week training program, due to the time he would be off the road. The problems with this type of an operation are numerous and all too common, and the result is time lost and double the intended investment. The following situation is an example of problems which arise when a department tries to cut corners financially.

Case Study

An officer who was having a problem with his dog contacted me. His department had purchased a dog and sent it to a private training facility to train. When the dog's training was complete, the officer attended a three-week handler course to learn how to work with the dog. He sent me a video to view and after giving him some recommendations, I stated my doubts about the dog's ability to be street workable.

The team hit the streets and had problems almost immediately. The officer who was handling the dog had never worked dogs before. As a result he had to trust in the judgment of the facility his department hired to evaluate and train his dog. He had no concept of how to work out the problems on his own. He had not been through a complete training program that taught him how to evaluate problems and train the dog. He had only learned the rudimentary concepts of how to handle an already trained animal.

The dog worked a year on the street but never made any physical contact with any suspect. His tracking ability was excellent, but his lack of will to make physical contact or fight suspects caused the handler genuine concern. In speaking with me he advised of a situation which occurred that he felt was quite serious. The dog had abandoned him during a dangerous confrontation with a suspect, failing him entirely. The officer was concerned that if he reported to his administration that the dog was unworkable, the program would be shut down. In this case, the dog was removed from the program and the officer was sent on another training program with a new dog.

Private Agencies

Many dogs sold throughout North America to police K9 programs are imported from overseas suppliers by private agencies. When the dog arrives in the United States or Canada, the importing agent often has no knowledge of the history of the animal. Since the demand for police dogs is great, these agencies often locate, train and sell dogs very quickly. Even with minimum turn around time, the agencies are unable to keep up with the demand for dogs. Fortunately most companies are reputable and put the proper time into the dog before placing the dog with a law enforcement agency.

Handler Candidates

Once the dog is ready, the police department then sends a candidate officer for training.

Often the officer is chosen because he has exhibited the most interest in the program, or because he is a high producer on the street. These qualifications do not always make a good dog handler. Although the officer has the desire, he might not have the type of personality to become a good handler. An experienced dog trainer will be able to help in making that judgment.

The officer who attends a brief program obtains the minimum amount of training required to handle the dog. Through no fault of the training agency, he receives a small portion of the training he really requires. This is a direct result of time constraints placed upon him.

As a result of these limitations the officer can only learn basic handling skills. There is not enough time to teach him how to train a dog. Any experienced K9 officer knows an officer cannot properly work a dog without adequate basic training as a foundation. When a training problem such as control work comes forth at a later date, the officer has no concept of how to correct it properly. His only recourse is to return to the training centre to remedy the problem. This takes the team off the road again and is a further added expense for the department. If the problem is ignored because the department cannot afford to send the officer for remedial work, they are exposed to possible lawsuit. It is not hard to see why a short handler's course with a pre-trained dog might not be suitable.

Abbreviated programs are ideal for officers who have previously completed a full training program and have worked a dog on the street for a number of years. They can take advantage of the reduced training time and at the same time be upgraded in their training.

Training vs. Handling

There is a distinct difference between *training* a dog and *handling* a dog. A well-trained dog can be handled by giving it appropriate direction and working with the animal. However, an officer cannot train a dog simply by learning how to handle it.

A good dog handler must understand how his dog thinks and how to read and understand the dog's behavior language. He must have a full understanding of how he can communicate with his dog and how his dog communicates with him. This is a prerequisite to the officer's tactical training, as everything the dog does tells the officer about the situation. Subtle body movements can indicate imminent danger to the well trained officer. The only way to learn the skills required to communicate with his partner adequately is for the officer to train the dog from the start.

The officer needs to learn how to select an untrained dog. He then learns to temperament test the dog for law enforcement use and how to train him. Upon completing a full program the officer then has the ability to work on most problems that arise in the dog's performance, without having to return to the agency where the dog was purchased.

Full Training Programs

If an officer starts to encounter training problems with his dog, the only recourse many departments have is corrective training at the facility where the dog was acquired. The agency that sold the dog employs qualified trainers who can work out the problems with the dog and return the team back to duty, but this is not productive or cost-effective.

Placing the officer through a full training program is a long term savings and produces teams that are superior on the street to those who have only received a basic handlers program. A full training program also allows the officer to learn advanced tactical training crucial to a K9 team. I cannot stress enough the need for full and proper training that includes officer survival techniques. A successful team will encounter more armed suspects and be at a higher risk simply because of its success rate. Therefore, it is reprehensible to deny a team appropriate training.

If you are going to use a private vendor, send your officer to a training facility which offers a full training program – one which allows him to learn how to train the dog from the basics up.

Apprehension Techniques

Reasonable Force vs. Handler Control

With the debate over standard handler-control training, as opposed to reasonable-force work, the dangers of civil litigation have become more complex. Reasonable force, which is also referred to as minimum force or circle and bark, has stirred up a lot of controversy about how police dogs are used in our society. It is a fallacy that using reasonable-force dogs alleviates lawsuits.

Numerous lawsuits have been launched from police dog applications involving victims who have been needlessly attacked by service dogs. Although the lawsuit may be the result of a dog bite, the handler's judgment and training will be the focal point of attorneys' cross-examinations. When there is justification for K9 application, every court in North America to date has upheld the use of handler-control techniques.

Reasonable-force dogs, both in theory and in practice in some departments, perform very well as street dogs. They sustain a low "bite ratio" on suspects, which appeals to department administrations. However, many hours of training are required for reasonable-force dog teams in order to keep the dogs sufficiently clean. This means if the training is not both proper and consistent, the dog will begin to bite in street applications when not warranted.

Agencies who buy pretrained Schutzhund-based dogs will be more susceptible to training difficulties and have a high risk for liability. Schutzhund dogs are trained for sporting events, with an emphasis on control work. This training is done in a sterile, cut and dried type of environment where the dog is conditioned to perform with exactly the same response in every situation. The scenarios never change and the same response is expected of the dog in each situation. Street situations are different with every application of a dog. The conditioning done in Schutzhund training, if extended into the advanced phases of training, causes difficulties when the dog must be converted to police work application. With the diversities required for police work, the police trainer frequently has to "untrain" the dog to make him useful for police work. If the dog is at an advanced level of Schutzhund training, this retraining of the dog can be difficult, and in times of real life applications the dog may revert back to its original training. This return to the basics first learned by the dog during Schutzhund training can mean a deadly situation on the street.

When purchasing potential candidates, Schutzhund-based dogs are excellent prospects for police work if acquired before training has passed beyond a Schutzhund I level. Anything over that can create specific difficulties for the law enforcement trainer. If your department has mandated a reasonable force policy, contact an agency that is running a successful police-oriented reasonable force program based on the German police methods of training. Two excellent training programs at the time of this writing are run by Wendell Nope at the Utah POST Academy in Salt Lake City, Utah and Terry Rogers of the Denver Police Department K9 Unit.

Theory of Reasonable Force

The theory of reasonable-force dogs maintains that if a suspect gives up, the dog will not bite, and that the dog is frequently in the position to make the decision whether or not to bite. Depending on the level of basic training and the amount of in-service work, this may or may not be true.

The dog has no ability to reason out a decision as to what the suspect's intentions are. The dog will only react to circumstances for which he has been conditioned. If improperly conditioned, he will bite when it is not warranted, or will not bite when needed the most. No trainer could possibly condition a dog for every conceivable action or reaction it will encounter on the street. This imposes limitations on the reasonable-force teams.

A handler using handler-control methods of apprehension, given the same set of circumstances as a reasonable-force dog, will direct his dog to bite only when necessary. If circumstances do not warrant a bite, the handler calls the dog off the attack, orders the dog to guard the suspect and proceeds with the arrest.

With a reasonable-force dog, when circumstances warrant a bite, the dog will also bite and hold onto the suspect until called off by the handler. If the situation does not warrant a bite, the dog continues to harass the suspect until the officer intervenes to make the arrest.

With the handler-control technique, the decision to have the dog physically apprehend a suspect by biting is made by the handler, who must remain within sight of his dog. The reasonable-force dog, on the other hand, makes that decision on his own, according to a perceived threat, if not under the direct supervision of a handler.

A dog which does not work under the direct supervision of the handler is the key difference between a reasonable-force dog and a handler-controlled dog, which is always under direct supervision by its handler. The marketing of reasonable-force methods seems in retrospect to be a strategy which has been sold to administrations to compensate for past problems. Instead of writing appropriate policies, being more cautious in the choice of handlers, keeping abreast of the latest training techniques and holding handlers accountable for their actions and applications of their dogs, the trend has been more towards allowing the dog to make the decision and training him not to bite unless the suspect shows an obvious physical form of aggression or escape. Unfortunately, not all suspects who use deadly force on police dogs and officers do so in such an aggressive manner that a reasonable-force dog can discern the intent in enough time to avert tragedy.

Bite Ratios

Statistical analysis of "bite ratios" can be deceptive. They can be manipulated to produce whatever results the researcher wishes to yield. Statistics produced comparing one agency to another do not often compare other mitigating circumstances. The level of crime rate might not be comparable. The number of violent suspects located as opposed to the number of property crime suspects located who did not resist arrest might not be included in the information.

The most recent report I have seen was published by the research and development office of a major city police department. The agency was doing research to determine if they should change their policy from bite-and-hold to reasonable-force applications. The research involved a comprehensive questionnaire sent to various departments regarding their policies and procedures. Agencies using both methods of apprehension were queried. Information was requested regarding any lawsuits against those departments arising from dog apprehensions. There were surprisingly few to report. However, at the time there were more lawsuits against reasonable-force departments than against handler control. It should be noted that the agency which conducted the research has, to date, stayed with its handler-control policy.

Liability

The liability for any dog bite rests on the shoulders of the handler, his supervisors and the department. For this reason, policy must be written which details under what circumstances a dog may be deployed and what procedures the officer must then follow. In general terms, this policy states that the officer's use of force with his dog must be within reasonable-force guidelines and within the laws governing that jurisdiction. Officer safety, along with public safety, must be the foremost consideration.

Documentation on each application must be detailed and complete. The extent of injury and the circumstances leading up to the application of the dog, as well as medical follow up treatment for the victim, needs to be recorded.

Liability is certainly no greater on a dog bite than on the misuse of a handgun, baton, or any other form of control device used by law enforcement. The application of these weapons must follow strict SOP guidelines within any department.

Minimizing Liability

Both handler-control and reasonable-force training styles have merit. If you have mandated reasonable-force applications, keep in mind they will not minimize liability any more than a properly trained handler-control team. Regardless of what method of apprehension techniques is applied, the potential for lawsuits remains the same. Liability can only be minimized when the dog is applied using clearly defined standard operating procedure, enforced by close supervision and documentation.

K9 Applications For Emergency Response Team

Integrating K9 Teams and ERT

In today's law enforcement there is a need for the use of police dogs in ERT applications. Many pro-active departments use the K9 team in ERT situations as an integral part of their operations. Sadly, however, many more departments have tried incorporating dogs into their ERT training only to have the programs fail miserably.

There are many ideas and differences of opinion amongst departments about the applications of dogs in emergency response tactics. Some departments excel in their combined operations. Others fail to such a degree that their administrators state they would never try to combine K9 and ERT again.

From an experienced K9 handler's point of view the answers are very simple. To an administrator or tactical team member who has only a basic knowledge of how a dog works, these answers can be hard to comprehend.

To dispel any misconception an officer may have regarding ERT and K9, the simple fact is that K9 can be a very useful and integral part of an ERT team. There are limitations, and to be successful every administrator, K9 handler and team member must be aware of them.

Law enforcement agencies who decide to use K9 teams with ERT must be very careful about how they approach their programs. A good patrol dog team does not necessarily make a good team for dynamic door entries.

> One of the major reasons K9 and ERT programs fail is due to the improper choice of the team.

Any good K9 handler will have an interest in working with ERT. It is an exciting challenge which offers a chance to become more diversified. Any dog handler I have met thrives on the action which comes from working the dog. Often, however, this can get in the way of making objective decisions about whether the team is the right one for the job. A few guidelines might be the easiest way to give a better insight into preparing for K9 applications in tactical situations.

Guidelines

When evaluating your needs for a specialized team, set down a guideline of what you will expect the team to do. Once your goals are set, then thoroughly meet each one. Obtain assistance from experts who have experience in the field.

Choose your K9 handler as you would any other team member. First, he must be trained as thoroughly as every other member in all aspects of tactical work. Do not choose a new K9 handler, or expect to put a fresh dog straight into ERT. The better choice is an experienced K9 officer with a seasoned dog.

The handler chosen must know his own limitations as well as those of his dog. He must also know when not to apply the dog just as he knows when and how to apply his dog.

> To use a dog when the situation makes it tactically unsound, simply to make use of the dog, is an invitation to disaster.

The handler must know when to back out of a situation and be allowed to do so. In all circumstances, the final decision to deploy the dog must always be left up to the handler.

Choice of Dog

The proper choice of dog is vital to the success of any program. The temperament of the animal must be such that he will be under maximum control of the handler in any circumstances, with a minimum of direction. A seasoned dog who shows stability under gunfire and restraint until directed into action by the handler makes an excellent candidate. The handler must be able to keep the dog silent and in many circumstances control the dog through hand signals for specific movements, without ever having to worry about the animal voicing. The element of surprise is lost should the suspect hear the dog bark while the team is setting up. This control can come only from proper preparation and the choice of an appropriate team.

> Never, under any circumstances send your K9 teams to work in a serious situation with your ERT team unless they have trained together.

Using the K9 teams to secure the outer perimeter during ERT operations should be the only use of any team which has not trained as an integral part of the team.

Use of K9 Teams

Door Entries

The uses of the dog in ERT situations are very diversified. The risk of any K9 being killed during a ERT operation is very high if he is used for door entries. To lose any dog is a great loss, however to lose a dog that regularly works the streets as a patrol dog can be an even greater loss. Not only would the department lose a specialty dog for ERT, they would also lose a dog that is used daily for patrol. The circumstances of each case must be evaluated and the risks considered and carefully weighed before deploying the K9. Under no circumstances is a dog a replacement for a simple waiting game on a barricaded gunman. Where circumstances without the dog do not warrant entry, neither do they warrant an entry simply because a K9 team is available. This is an unnecessary risk.

Barricaded Suspects

During any barricaded situation your K9 teams can be used for outer perimeter containment should a suspect somehow manage to escape through the inner perimeter. A fleeing felon is an easy mark for a well trained team. At night the dog can often indicate to the handler when someone is on the move, even though the target is not visible. As the dog hears or smells the suspect the handler is alerted to possible target movement in circumstances where the suspect is trying to move out under the cover of darkness. If circumstances warrant applying the dog to check out the indication, the dog is released to neutralize the subject. This is particularly useful in open field searches for known armed suspects.

Where an armed suspect is barricaded in a building and negotiations are continuing, the use of any intervention by force is questionable as long as negotiations are effective. Circumstances must dictate whether the dog's life should be risked, as opposed to simply waiting the offender out. Once the decision has been made, the dog's action must be swift, accurate and sure. There is no time to reconsider your options. It is essential that the team is rapid and effective. Any hesitation by the animal is likely to result in violent repercussions. When use of a dog fails, it closes any doors which have been opened through negotiation. The proper application of the dog must be in co-ordination with an entry team that will enter the building whether the dog is successful or not.

Suicidal Suspects

Where a subject is threatening suicide and continually pointing a weapon at himself, a dog team is often considered. The catch to these circumstances is that many of these subjects are passive. For this reason, the dog must be capable of taking down and disarming a passive suspect as effectively as an aggressive suspect.

Reasonable-force dogs should not be used for ERT team applications, or applied on passive suspects. Handler-control dogs trained to attack passive suspects are preferred in these situations. The use of reasonable-force dogs has resulted in the loss of good dogs as well as loss of human life when improperly applied in seemingly passive circumstances.

Case Study

Kansas City, Missouri lost one of its finest dogs during a K9 application into a house, going after an armed suspect who was wanted for the attempted murder of a police officer. Tactical teams deployed on the house and the handler deployed the dog to search for the suspect after calling out warnings into the residence. The dog located the suspect and immediately went into a reasonable force type of indication by barking at the suspect instead of attacking, even though the suspect was within reach. The suspect fired two shots into the dog. Although the dog managed to pull his way back to his handler, and was rushed to a nearby veterinary clinic, he died of his injuries.

Suspect Location

Service dogs can be used to locate a gunman in a building using a stealth approach. Backed up by ERT, the officer places his dog on long line. The building is then searched for any hiding places the suspect could be. When the dog indicates a location the ERT team is advised to secure that area. The search then continues to ensure there are no more suspects, or the suspect has not moved prior to the first indication of the dog. This is an accurate method of detecting where the suspect is concealed and pinpoints the location for the team to work on. At this point the dog team takes up a position of rear security and containment and allows ERT to do its job, now the specific location of the suspect has been determined.

CS/CN Gas Conditions

The dog team is also used on door entries. The dog is not affected to a great degree by the use of CS or CN munitions and is a powerful tool under gas conditions. Once an area has been secured and the appropriate amount of chemical agent applied, the dog is deployed into the area to locate and disarm the suspect.

Training profiles show most dogs lose no effectiveness in their olfactory capabilities and are very capable of searching for offenders in gas conditions. Experiments where the dog worked in CN or CS gas to search for hidden articles or suspects resulted in the dog being successful on every occasion with little or no side effects. The smoke used in tactical operations is a problem however, and the dogs must be trained in these environments extensively before being applied in live situations. Keep this capability in mind should you need to clear a building of any further possible suspects after an operation.

2
Patrol Officer's Guide to K9

Introduction To Patrol Officers

The line officer needs to understand the versatility of the dog section and be aware of how he can best work with that team. Police dogs are an effective resource at your disposal when pursuing fleeing suspects, searching for stolen property, locating and recovering evidence at crime scenes, or apprehending armed and dangerous persons.

Deployment of the K9 unit is a team effort. This cannot be stressed enough. Patrol Officers are as important to the successful application of the dog as the dog team itself. Without proper backup and containment by patrol officers the chances for a successful conclusion to any K9 application is reduced. Proper containment and scene preservation by patrol can increase the K9 team's success rate as much as 30 to 40 percent.

How The Dog Works

Any dog has a powerful ability to detect and analyze odors. He also has a strong ability to store and recall specific odors which he has imprinted on his memory. The police service dog is conditioned to use those abilities to detect specific odors.

Physiology

When looking closely at the inner structure of the dog's nose, the area on each side of the nasal septum is a maze of tiny structures called the *turbinate bones*. These scroll-like passages are covered on both sides with membranes that detect odor. This area of the dog's nose, the area where odors are first detected, is many times more effective than that of a human.

The dog also has a gland in the roof of the mouth, between the upper canine teeth called the *vomeronasal gland*. This gland is connected to the olfactory portion of the dog's brain and has the ability to detect tasted scent. This gives the dog the ability to detect odor which it in fact tastes, such as with bloodhounds. In police dog applications it helps the dog to track a fresh scent very rapidly by taking odor in through the mouth.

When the dog gets close to a suspect, the dog lifts his head and begins to work the odor through his mouth. This is a strong indicator to the handler that the suspect is nearby and a warning that he should prepare for possible confrontation.

Tunnel Scent

When working with his head up, showing excitement and tracking at an increased intensity, the dog is following what is called the *tunnel scent* of the suspect. Tunnel scent is odor left airborne behind a suspect as he flees. This odor drops off the suspect in a cone-like formation and in effect leaves a trail for the dog to follow.

Each person's scent is as unique and individual as a fingerprint. Ethnic origin, health, the type of foods the person eats and the soaps and perfumes he wears all make up the odor which is individual to that person. The type of clothing worn and the articles the person carries also make up the scent. His body contact with articles such as stolen property or discarded weapons also affords the dog the ability to recover articles specific to the individual.

Windborne Scent

Windborne scent from a discarded object can originate from this previous human contact, or may also be characteristic of the object itself. For example, a dog can easily detect a purse discarded in a bush area if he is worked downwind, as the scent of the leather will attract the dog's attention. It is foreign to the surrounding area and as a result the dog will lead its handler to the article. In this way a dog can be used to search and recover articles which are discarded hours and even days before.

This method has succeeded, in thousands of cases, and has many varied applications. Another good use of this type of application is to search for discarded shell casings or bullets at a crime scene. The dog can easily detect credit cards discarded in heavy shrubbery or tall grass. These are all instances where the dog is using the windborne scent.

Scent Trails

What about situations where the airborne scent has been dispersed by winds or other disturbances? Wherever a person goes, whether he is sitting, standing, walking, running, or even swimming, he sheds thousands of minute particles of skin called rafts. These rafts of skin contain the person's individual genetic scent composition. As these rafts of skin fall off a person, they come into contact with the surrounding area. They may fall onto nearby plants, onto the pavement or sidewalk, or may be rubbed off onto a nearby wall. Again, this is another form of trail for the dog to follow.

As the suspect flees, he also runs across various surfaces. When he disturbs these surfaces, new fresh odors are released, making a trail for the dog. A crushed insect or vegetation releases fresh scents for the dog to work with. This is known as *ground scent*.

Another form of scent, called *contact scent,* is odor which transfers from one surface to another. As the suspect flees across a grass surface, thousands of microscopic particles are picked up on his shoes. As he proceeds onto a sidewalk, these particles are deposited along his trail, and he now picks up minute particles of lime and other products which make up the sidewalk. As he continues to a paved surface, he continues to leave small particles from the grass surface, as well as particles from the sidewalk. He now comes into contact with a surface which will leave small particles of tar and oil residue on his shoes which will also transfer to the next surface.

This process of transfer, the freshly disturbed ground scent and the odor left behind on rafts of skin from the suspect, all give a detectable and continuous trail to the dog.

Track Contamination

A dog has one more very strong asset. The olfactory lobe of the brain enables him to readily discriminate scent. Although the track may become contaminated by other people walking through the area, the dog can sort out scents that are interfering with the original track and work the track to a successful conclusion.

The more contamination that occurs in an area, however, the more difficult it is for the dog to work the available scent. As people walk through the offender's path, the scent which he has left behind him is disturbed. These disturbances can often blow the scent in various directions. This can cause the dog to go the wrong direction and often lose the track. If the dog is working well and the conditions are good, however, the dog still may work the track out.

Even though the dogs have this ability, it makes the chance for a successful track less likely. Thus, it is up to the patrol officer at the scene to contain and preserve the area to the best of his ability. If there are other scents at the crime scene, the dog will not know which scent is the suspect's. You must keep the crime scene clear from other persons' scent until the dog team has arrived and a track has been initiated.

Backing Up The Dog Team

Patrol Officers must be capable of escorting the dog handler on any call. This is vital. Most K9 officers are shot and killed or gravely injured because at the time of the confrontation they were without a backup.

Patrol Officer's Role

As a K9 Officer's backup you become a part of the K9 team. If you cannot meet the physical challenges faced by the K9 team, then be certain someone who is capable assists as a backup. When working as a backup to the dog unit, you must be prepared to keep up to your handler under any circumstance. Many officers drop out of the chase when they must start jumping fences, or when the area gets muddy and their uniform starts to get soiled. We instinctively slow down and pick our way through muddy areas to stay as clean as possible, as dress and deportment is drilled into us from the first days in the academy. When escorting the dog handler however, you must shed your natural inhibitions and stay with him. You are vital to his safety.

The K9 Officer must concentrate on his dog and if working on line, cannot have his weapon out at the ready should a confrontation suddenly occur. It is the patrol officer's responsibility to stay with your dog handler and prepared to handle such a situation, should it occur.

Positioning

Psychological data and track statistics have shown most suspects conceal themselves on the right side of a track. As a backup officer, you should place yourself about twenty feet behind the dog handler and about ten feet to his right, the five o'clock position. This places you the furthest distance from the suspect once the dog locates him, but is still within effective range of your sidearm.

Proper backup officer position using one officer.

This configuration allows for an adequate spread between you and the handler and allows you the best possibility of a clear field of fire at most suspects. Officers who back up the K9 team by positioning themselves directly behind the handler at the six o'clock position are unable to give adequate cover to the area in front of the handler. By using the five o'clock escort procedure, you force the suspect to deal with the dog as well as two officers, all at different angles and distances. The psychological advantage is tremendous

Backup positions when two officers are available.

and will often cause the suspect to change his mind about engaging in a gunfight.

If there are two backup officers, proper positioning is with one officer in the five o'clock position from the K9 team and the secondary backup officer at the seven o'clock position. This allows both backup officers maximum fields of fire in both directions. In a serious situation where you have the benefit of three backup officers, the third officer can take the six o'clock position, about ten feet farther behind the handler than the other two officers. Again, this provides for maximum coverage from all officers without much concern about crossfire should the suspect decide to engage in a firefight.

There are two situations you should be particularly aware of when working as a backup officer. The first arises during tracks of fleeing suspects.

Potential Ambush

First, when tracking, the dog can often get into situations where he is very close to the suspect, but continues by him because the wind is coming in a direction which causes the scent to drift away from the area. This can be extremely dangerous to the dog handler, since by the time the dog realizes he has overshot the suspect, the handler is well within the suspect's kill zone. This is the reason for the distance between you and your K9 handler and the reason you must be alert to potential ambush. If the suspect is armed, it is likely he will be waiting to ambush the dog team. You must be aware of the risk and prepare yourself to handle the situation with immediate and decisive action.

The psychological difference between having a backup officer on the track or working alone can be a deciding factor in an offender's decision to shoot.

Building Searches

The second major area of concern occurs during building searches. Similar to scent which can deceive the dog into momentarily overshooting the suspect on a track is a phenomenon in building searches commonly called the *chimney effect*. This is where the suspect's scent rises to the ceiling, travels across the room, or into the next aisle in a warehouse and then floats back to the ground, directly opposite to where the suspect is actually hiding.

The dog works the scent, but because of this phenomenon, a strong portion of the scent is away from the suspect's location.

> Use extreme caution in building searches when escorting the dog handler.

Maintain adequate distance and use all the caution a street officer would if he were searching the building without the assistance of a K9 team.

Remember, because human scent can travel with air currents and rise and fall in the atmosphere according to temperature, the suspect may in fact be behind you or your dog handler when the dog is working the scent in an area in front of you. Given proper time, the handler will be able to get the dog to work to the source of the scent. Be prepared to back him up until the dog closes in on the suspect's true location.

Case Study

In January of 1981, Officer Kevin O'Shaugnessy of the King County Police Department in Washington State was called to assist a neighboring agency in the search for a bank robbery suspect. The suspect had fled in a vehicle which he later dumped in a rural area. Patrol officers spotted the abandoned car and requested King County's dog for assistance.

The call came in late in the day and it was near dusk when Officer O'Shaugnessy arrived at the scene. Initially it was not known exactly how many suspects were involved and two backup officers were chosen to cover O'Shaugnessy on the track.

O'Shaugnessy released his dog to track and soon found himself working in heavy bush. He was in an unfamiliar area and depended on the two backup officers for assistance. During the track, the two officers tried to follow trails through the heavy bush, instead of staying with the K9 team. It was not long before O'Shaugnessy found himself alone, on an intense track, without any backup and having no idea of the area, or where he was.

About 30 minutes into the track, K9 Jake started to show intensity, giving indications he was closing on the suspect. They entered a small clearing about fifteen feet in diameter and the dog suddenly keyed on a bush area across the clearing and went in for the attack. In that instant the suspect opened fire from his position with a .357 magnum. Jake was shot once in the head and once in the chest, dropping instantly. O'Shaugnessy never saw the gunman. He too was hit. Once in the left arm and another round that entered his stomach between the panels of his vest. He returned fire in the direction of where he thought the gunshots had come from as he got back to cover. He thought he had fired four rounds and was going to take the opportunity to reload while he had a chance, now that he was behind adequate cover. In fact, he had fired five rounds. Before he could reload, the suspect started screaming to O'Shaugnessy that he had counted the officers shots and knew he was out of ammunition. He was going to come and kill him. O'Shaugnessy knew he had at least one round left and there was no time to attempt a reload. He watched as the suspect started to get up from his position and fired one round into the suspect's chest, successfully neutralizing him.

Officer Kevin O'Shaugnessy and K9 Jake. In O'Shaugnessy's incident both backup teams fell behind. The officer, dog and offender all received gunshot wounds in the ensuing gun battle.

O'Shaugnessy was in an area he was unfamiliar with, unable to give adequate directions to surrounding units. He, his dog and the suspect were all wounded by gunfire. He depended heavily on his backup, primarily because he was assisting another agency in an area he was not familiar with. Now he had to try and direct other members to his location to get assistance.

After the incident was over, medics brought in a backboard to carry out the dog and O'Shaugnessy managed to walk out on his own power. As they approached the ambulance, his dog suddenly lifted his head and looked around. Up until this point the officer had thought his dog was dead. Although the dog was knocked unconscious by the bullet to the head, he survived the impact of the bullet. It did not penetrate the skull and had lodged just under the skin behind the ears.

The suspect also survived this incident. Investigation revealed he had taken the time to find a clearing where he could see the officers come through if he was pursued. He had taken a full box of ammunition with him. Upon deciding where he would make his stand, the suspect pulled out the box and placed it on a log in front of him, open and easily accessible for reloading. When the officer approached, the suspect already had a plan in mind. His most immediate threat was the dog and he looked after that threat appropriately. He then followed through by attempting to kill the officer.

At the time of the incident, both escort officers were wearing their full dress uniforms, including hats and had armed themselves with shotguns. Their concern over keeping their uniforms clean took more precedent than staying with the dog handler. A shotgun, while a formidable weapon against an armed opponent is also unwieldy in heavy bush and likely inappropriate under the circumstances.

Appropriate Weaponry

If a track proceeds through heavy brush, consideration should be given as to whether you should employ the use of either a rifle or a shotgun. While the use of such weapons in heavy bush may be preferable, extra caution must be taken in your method of carrying the weapon. In working through extremely dense bush, carrying these weapons may slow you down, which in turn places your dog handler at risk. Your K9 handler will also feel a bit apprehensive if the officer behind him is using the weapon to swath through the bush.

This is not to say such weapons should not be taken on any tracks. In fact, there are circumstances where they are more appropriate specifically due to their ability to penetrate bush. The decision needs to be made according to each individual circumstance. An aid to carrying a shotgun or rifle in such circumstances would be the use of a tactical sling for the weapon.

After the incident O'Shaugnessy was advised he should have waited for the officers. As most K9 handlers know, it is not feasible to stop every few feet to wait for your backup officer. Had the officers assigned to escort the dog handler stayed with him, it is very likely the gunfight might never have occurred. A suspect is less likely to confront three officers and a dog than the K9 team alone.

Evidence Recovery

As the escorting officer you may also be responsible for maintaining any exhibits or evidence recovered by the dog. This evidence will be your responsibility, at the direction of the K9 handler. Try to secure these items where possible and if not, call in another unit to secure evidence so you can continue the track with the dog handler. Under no circumstances should the recovery of any evidence supersede your primary assignment, which is to cover the K9 officer.

Backtracks/Confirmation Tracks

An effective method of using your dog teams is to have them work backtracks for you. Often you may check suspects who you feel have just been involved in a crime. By getting assistance from the dog team, you can ask the handler to start a track from where the suspects were found and track back to where they have just come from. These tracks are usually very successful as the trail is fresh and makes for an easy success.

Narcotics Searches

Most departments use dogs which are cross trained for patrol and either narcotics or explosives. When stopping a vehicle, if you suspect you are confronting someone involved in the drug trade, a cursory search and positive indication by a dog may give enough probable grounds to obtain a warrant to search the vehicle. Depending on the individual laws of the area, it may not require anything more than reasonable grounds for a search. If such reasonable grounds exist, the dog can be used to search the vehicle to recover the contraband.

Communication Between Patrol and The K9 Officer

Awareness is the key in effective communication. Do not generalize in communications to fellow officers or K9 teams and make sure they acknowledge your information to be sure it is received. Be as specific as you can on circumstances and descriptions.

Identify what weapons if any were involved in the offense and the seriousness of the offense. What items were taken from the scene that the offender might drop along the way or still have in his possession when found? Remember, clothing can be discarded quickly and physical descriptors should be as detailed as possible about the individual himself as well as the clothing.

Cursory information can also be valuable in the recovery and identification of evidence. If the suspect was wearing gloves at the time of the offense, describe the gloves. Should the K9 officer's dog locate such an item during the track, the officer will be aware of it and retain it for evidence. Obtain details of the weapon used, type of mask or disguise and any other pertinent details which might assist the dog handler in recovering evidence on the track.

Two-way communication is a must. The escorting officer, or the K9 officer himself, must keep the containment team apprised. Direction of travel along with any information gleaned from the track, may be important to the containment team. When discarded clothing is located along the track, advise your surrounding officers so they are aware that the clothing of the suspect may be different from the original description. The following incident clearly illustrates how a lack of information can lead to fatal consequences.

Case Study

On July 16, 1986 at 0300 hours, an officer with the Anchorage Alaska Police Department observed a car without tail lights drive past her in the opposite direction. The officer negotiated a U turn and initiated a routine stop on the car. Unknown to the officer, the car's driver was a recently paroled felon who had robbed a bank earlier that day. He had also recently been the subject of a check while operating a motorcycle, and when stopped by police, had pulled a gun on the officer and fled. This time, as the officer approached the suspect exited the car with a handgun, pointed the gun at her and ordered her to "freeze." The officer jumped to the right into a ditch as the suspect opened fire. She returned fire as the suspect ran to the police vehicle and fled in her patrol car.

At the time, the offense was classified as an Assault Three, assault with a deadly weapon. Due to a hostage crisis that was also in progress, the only information provided over the radio at the time was the pursuit of an Assault Three suspect. In some cases, the officers only heard the word assault come over the air. Through all the confusion nobody seemed to be aware a gunfight had ensued prior to the theft of the patrol car. This lack of information may have played a major role in the death of one of the K9 officers.

K9 Officer Rick Giles started a track with his dog, backed up by K9 Officer Jim Hanson. The dog tracked the suspect into a bush area. As they approached, the suspect jumped over a fence and continued to run. When they closed on the suspect a second time, they saw him run into spruce bushes at the corner of a house lot. There was a fence at the back separating the lot from a roadway. Officer Giles released the dog to attack, but the dog had not seen the suspect enter the bush area and reverted to searching for the suspect as the handler skirted around the end of the fence. As the dog entered the bush in pursuit of the suspect, Officer Hanson bent down to follow the dog into the bush and was shot. He was killed instantly by the suspect's bullet.

After the suspect killed Officer Hanson, he jumped over the fence to escape the dog. This brought him onto the roadway where he was confronted by Officer Giles. Another gunfight ensued with Giles shooting at the suspect four times and striking him four times. One round entered the pelvis of the suspect and knocked him down, however he did not cease his actions at that time. He continued until shot again and finally physically subdued by another officer.

No one knew until the incident was over the suspect had been involved in a gunfight during the initial traffic stop. As a result of poor communications, the two K9 officers had no idea the suspect they were pursuing was armed. Had they known this, it is quite likely Officer Hanson might not have been so quick to follow the dog into the bushes.

Do not assume those you pursue are unarmed. The one time you let down your guard will be the one time you come face to face with a weapon.

Containment

Patrol officers responding to an area must remember containment has two purposes. The primary function is to force the suspects to "go to ground." When setting up co-ordinates for containment, you must always be conscious of the time delays involved. If the crime is on view, reported in progress as you approach the scene, then you know you can set your containment up within a tighter perimeter. On the other hand, if it is a silent alarm, there is a good chance the suspects are in and out of the target area before the alarm company gets the call through to your dispatch and the call is in turn dispatched to you. When you consider your response time to the scene, the suspects could be at least six blocks in any direction before you arrive. The major mistake officers doing containment make is setting up too close to the scene.

Procedure

1. Once into position, illuminate every emergency light and spotlight you have available. Let the suspects know you are there so they will not try to break through the containment. Force them to go to ground and wait for the dog team. If you feel you are at risk and exposed by staying in your patrol car, secure the vehicle and exit to a secure vantage point. If you know the suspects are armed and feel you may be at risk staying in the car, set up the area you want lit up. Exit your car to an area of cover where you can observe the target area and still maintain control over your vehicle.

2. The second function of containment is to keep other people from entering the area being searched. This is for their own safety and to prevent them from adding more scent to the area in which the dog has to work. Do not hesitate to stop cars from driving over a road the suspects are likely to cross. This will prevent cars from driving over any possible track left by the suspect.

3. Exhaust from cars, especially those equipped with catalytic converters, is particularly detrimental to the dog's sense of smell. It has a numbing effect on the dog's olfactory system and although it is only a brief hindrance, it can mean the difference between a successful and unsuccessful application. Whenever you are parked near where the dog team is working or beside a K9 unit, shut down your engine.

4. Never drive your car down an alley following your dog team on a track. Should the dog overshoot the scent, the handler must return to the point where the dog had last indicated the track. Officers who drive over the track after the dog team has gone by destroy this point of reference. Give them some time before driving over any known track, to be certain the handler does not need to reapply his dog in the area.

5. When the dog team tracks past the outer perimeter of your containment cars and it becomes obvious the suspects have gone past the point of outer containment, then expand your perimeters in an attempt to box them in again. For example, if the suspects are moving north from the crime scene and they have broken through the northern most perimeter, have any cars south of that point move up into new areas of containment and set up new perimeters. The northern-most patrol units now become the southern edge of the perimeter since they never leave their original positions. This prevents the suspects from doubling back should these cars clear the area. It is not unusual for suspects to go to ground to catch their breath just outside the contained area, because they managed to get that far before the perimeter was set up.

6. Remember, the faster a perimeter of containment is set up, the better the chances are the dog will make an arrest. His success is as dependent on your efforts as on his own abilities. You must work together as a team to be successful.

Car Accidents Involving The K9 Unit

With the ever increasing rate which dogs are called to crimes, there is a greater risk of the K9 unit being involved in a serious car accident. Situations have occurred where units arriving on the scene are unable to assist an injured K9 officer because he is trapped inside his car, with his confused and excited dog instinctively protecting him from those who are there to help. There is concern that a good service dog might be destroyed by attending officers trying to gain entry to the vehicle. This type of tragedy can be avoided in most situations. The first officer on the scene should immediately call another K9 unit for assistance. Another K9 Officer can give instructions which will help considerably.

If the injured officer is conscious, tell him to close the separator between the front and rear compartment (if the car is equipped with one). If the officer is not capable of assisting you can usually gain access to the front compartment of the car long enough to reach in and close the separator by having a second officer tease and distract the dog from the opposite side of the car.

Products issued for subduing suspects can also be used in an emergency, if necessary. Incapacitating sprays which are capsicum based will effectively subdue the dog; however, keep in mind the residue will also affect other rescuers and the officer who is still in the vehicle.

If it becomes necessary to remove the dog from the car the officer's spouse or another family member who is familiar with the dog can be brought to the scene. There is usually someone close to the officer who can properly handle the dog. The best available resource person in all cases is another dog handler. He will be able to effectively handle the situation. The first course of action should always be to contact the nearest available dog handler and get him to the scene.

Common sense prevails in all cases. The dog is very much a part of the handler's family and is his best friend on the road, not to mention the fact he is an asset to the department. He will be confused and excited in such a situation, so stay rational. You will likely arrive at a successful conclusion for which your dog handler and his family will be always grateful.

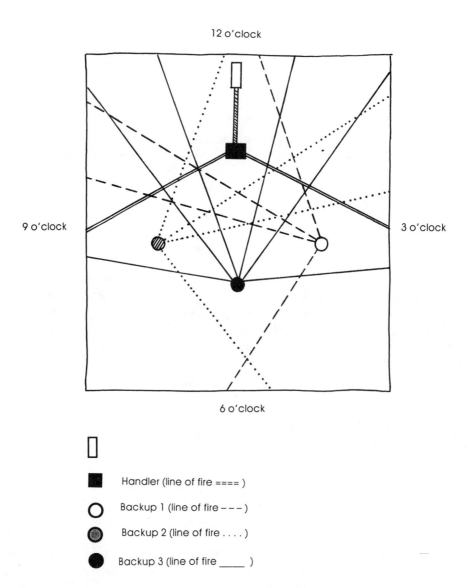

3

3
K9 Officers

Introduction To K9 Officers

The career you have chosen is not a game. Don't take unnecessary risks. Know what your personal limitations are as well as those of your K9 partner.

> If in any doubt about an application, don't do it. Too often officers take on tasks beyond their limitations because they feel a personal obligation to do so.

If you are asked to perform a dangerous assignment which you and your dog are trained and prepared for, then handle the situation accordingly. Refuse assignments you have not trained for. Do not feel compelled to perform because you are the only K9 officer available at the time. When you are not prepared for that type of situation, you are endangering yourself and the officers you are there to assist. You will have more respect from your peers and administration if you make proper judgment calls on your limitations than if you don't go home to your family at the end of the shift.

As you become experienced in the world of the Police K9, you will learn to read and understand the warning signals your dog gives you. You know what your partner is capable of and how he best applies his talents. You always have the final say in whether your dog should be applied in any situation and how the application should be made. Make your decisions carefully and concentrate on going home at the end of shift.

K9 teams work hours considered to be high-risk times, between 20:00 hours and 04:00 hours. During this period of time the K9 officer will be called upon to handle many routine tasks. However, he will also attend all high risk crimes which occur in his district.

Consider the facts. As a K9 officer you face more violent encounters as both the primary unit as well as the backup unit, on a more frequent basis than any other officer. You drive to incidents using emergency equipment and travel at high rates of speed in your unit more frequently than most officers. Your most active times of work are during the hours of darkness. You face suspects armed with weapons, who have already committed crimes and are trying to evade arrest. You are more prone to attack than most other officers.

As a direct result of your dog applications you often reengage suspects who have already had confrontations with the primary officers who attended the call and manage to escape. Due to the nature of your work you find yourself alone, without backup, facing one or more suspects who have the advantage of watching you approach.

Long before your shift begins, you must be mentally and physically prepared for any possible situation which you might face on the street. If you are not in the right frame of mind to handle virtually any type of incident you might be faced with during your shift, then you are putting yourself and those people who depend on you at risk. Know your capabilities and limitations. In this business, we can't afford to make mistakes.

The K9 Team Mission

The primary objective of the K9 team is to search for suspects or evidence linked to a specific crime scene. The dog is one of the many investigative tools the patrol team has available.

The support service provided by the dog section goes beyond the primary initiative in ways which are very effective. The dog can locate missing persons, detect illicit drugs or explosives. The team can back up patrol on calls where the dog's presence can have a psychological effect or where his physical abilities may deter or prevent violent confrontation.

Guidelines for K9 Officers

1. A good team must realize the purpose of the dog team is to serve as a support service for patrol officers. Your obligations are to your fellow members. Just as the identification section is a support service which responds to a crime scene at the request of a field officer, so follows the mandate of the dog handler. You are there to aid the field officer in locating evidence for a case or in tracking down a suspect who has left a crime scene under investigation. You cannot be successful as a dog handler without the support of patrol, and your credibility will go a long way in getting the assistance you need from them. There will be days when your dog is just not successful. Failure can depend on many variables – in most cases there is too much contamination and interference of the scent for the dog to work it successfully. There will be days when your dog is not up to it, as there are days when you get up and do not feel like going to work.

2. As a dog team, you are not out on the street to provide a form of "street justice" by mauling suspects. You are an effective means of locating and apprehending criminals. Your attitude and professionalism will be apparent in the manner you apply your dog. Be certain the crime for which you are deploying your dog is arrestable before setting the dog on a track. If there is any doubt at all, do not apply your dog in a manner which will allow him to make physical contact with the pursued subject.

3. Know your department policies on dog applications and adhere to those regulations. Those policies will provide you with job demands specifically tailored to your department's need and will guide you in your deployment. Following your department Standard Operating Procedures can also help protect you from criminal and civil liabilities.

4. Another function you must perform as a dog team is public demonstrations. This may seem unimportant, however it is important to the success of a good dog program, since it builds support from the public sector. This also brings positive media support which is necessary for any department wishing to have a successful dog section. Public awareness can be positive and supportive but it can also be destructive. The abandonment of a dog program can be surprisingly swift with the onset of bad press and negative public pressure.

Bruce Jackson, a K9 trainer with the Washington State Police K9 Association summed up the K9 mission as follows:

> *"Your mission is clear cut and well defined. The set of philosophies you develop in order to achieve that mission will determine whether you make a beneficial contribution to the role police dogs play in modern law enforcement or whether you become a liability which undermines the good work of many men before you."*

Stress Considerations – Officer And K9

The career of a police officer involves high stress levels. Officers are prone to heart attacks, high blood pressure and premature deaths as a direct result of the job. The stress an officer goes through also includes financial burdens, home difficulties and the other problems most people have. On top of these stressors, there are problems specific to the job, which make the officer's problems more complex to deal with.

Stress Levels

Through a period of a single shift, an officer's stress level will change many times. Internal pressures from a superior, being antagonized by a citizen when writing a citation and the sudden tone alert on the radio all contribute to the mental state of mind and stress level. These stresses are often intermingled with long periods of boredom, usually taken up by hours of report writing, or general patrol. When entering a situation which is perceived as serious, such as the track of a fleeing suspect, the heart rate increases with the apprehension of the chase, if even to a slight degree. The officer's apprehension will increase even more as his dog closes in on a suspect, and is further increased by physical activity, such as running and clearing fences.

In such a situation, it is not difficult to see the officer's physical and emotional condition is being exercised to capacity as he nears the end of the track. It is at this point he must often confront one or more offenders. Should a physical confrontation suddenly occur, or worse, a gunfight situation with one or more suspects, he must be able to mentally and physically handle the situation. If physically healthy and able to work extended tracks with a minimum of effort, he has one less concern when a confrontation occurs.

Officer Stress Reduction

Training conditions the handler to mentally prepare for potential problems. If he has prepared accordingly, his stress levels will be reduced. In turn, the ability to handle a situation is improved. By maintaining a strong physical fitness level he is better prepared to handle street situations and at the same time reduce his general level of stress. Just as an officer can maintain a level of physical fitness, his capabilities and confidence will be enhanced by training programs designed to teach conditioned responses.

K9 Stress

The dog has the same potential to be affected by stress in his activities. This stress can cause premature aging and illnesses. He may become irritable and lack enthusiasm when working. Advanced phases of stress can be indicated by uncontrollable shaking, nervousness or anxiety in certain situations.

The major testing phases of choosing a dog for suitability in law enforcement include stress tests. From the time the dog is a few weeks old, there is a series of tests which can be done to indicate whether the dog has the ability to handle the pressures of police service, or whether he should be rejected.

As the dog becomes more experienced on the street, he will encounter situations where he must deal with violent suspects after working extended tracks. He will meet more physical resistance from suspects armed with various weapons such as knives, guns, crowbars and tire irons.

In one case my service dog "Lance" was assaulted by a suspect who attacked him with a board filled with nails. One nail pierced his front knee, resulting in major surgery and three months of casting and physiotherapy before being returned to active duty. Despite his wounds, he still managed to take down the offender.

As we must be prepared for our job on the street, we must also keep our K9 partners fit to handle the stresses of the street. Choose a partner with good temperament and raise him in a manner which builds his drive and confidence. Build his natural skills, and through the bonding process instill the basics of trust and control into the animal. As your dog matures, continue to test him for his ability to handle stress.

Should you encounter a situation where the dog is incapable of handling stress, you should seek a new candidate. An animal which breaks down under stress will be unreliable in crucial situations. The dog responds to stress situations much like humans. His heart rate increases, he becomes more agitated and if there is too much stress for him to handle, he will break down.

The dog's responses en route to a call are physically similar to the officer's. Over a period of time he has learned when the speed of the patrol car increases, or when there is a burst of the siren, he is likely to get work. He will stand up in the car and show excitement by barking or pacing the rear of the car.

These external signs of excitement accompany mental and physiological changes. The blood pressure and heart rate increase as the dog anticipates the coming action. The increased adrenalin and mental activity which causes these physiological changes are all factors which increase the dog's stress level. The dog must handle this stressor as well as the stress of the track, obstacles and any possible violent encounter with the suspect. Throughout the incident he must remain confident and reliable.

Upon arrival, if K9 assistance is not required, the dog's anticipation will remain high until he realizes he will not be used. From this point the adrenalin flow decreases, in turn decreasing the blood pressure and heart rate. When he is not used he will feel let down, much in the same manner as if you had offered to play "fetch" with him and after working him up into a playful mood you suddenly put the ball away.

Throughout each shift a K9 team may deal with eight or ten calls resulting in differing decisions on using the dog. In a training scenario you can decide whether or not the dog gets his bite and can ensure a successful track. In service you may go days with incomplete tracks, or calls where your partner is never needed to assist. Such are the circumstances of the job.

Your partner must be capable of withstanding the pressures of constant variation. Added to the normal everyday stress of individual calls are the times where people intentionally tease the dog as they walk by the squad car. Add other such incidents and you have the potential for your partner to become stressed due to continual sudden changes in aggression and activity levels.

K9 Stress Reduction

During the dog's years of service on the street you must be aware of the effects of stress and do your best to help him handle it. Failure to do so may result in an excellent working dog becoming "burned out" years before his expected working life is over.

Easing the pressures of the job on your partner is actually a simple task. There are a few very simple exercises which you can do to decrease the dog's stress and fulfill his desire to please you as well.

1. After training is completed and you have hit the streets, your dog will require as much rest as you between shifts. When you build his kennel at home be sure it is in a secluded area where he will not be distracted by outside influences. He must be able to rest sufficiently and know he can remain relaxed within his domain without having to be prepared for anything. He also needs time to be alone and relax without interference from children. Therefore, on days where you are sleeping between nightshifts it may be preferable to bring the dog into your room to rest. This way you are sure he will not be bothered and will be rested adequately for the following nightshift.

2. Maintain his health and ensure he is fed on a strict schedule. Shiftwork can play havoc with the dog's physiological functions as easily as man's. Should

his sleeping, feeding and activity patterns be irregular and sporadic you will be adding unnecessary stress onto his physical health.

3. Next on the list is maintaining his activity rate on the streets with some form of playtime after an incomplete call. His anxiety has built up while en route to various calls and he is eager to work. You can fulfill his need to complete the task by playing with him after an incomplete call. A game of tug of war, fetching a ball, a short area search or track will do wonders to vent the dogs anxiety and fulfill his need to work. He will also learn every incomplete call is not necessarily a let down. Keep the exercises simple and short so you are fulfilling his desire to complete the task without making him work too hard for it. This is a cooling down exercise and one does not want to keep his stress level up or tire him so he is unable to work on a difficult or lengthy call.

4. Finally, on your days off be certain to spend adequate amounts of time with your partner to maintain his skills and fulfill his desire to work for you. Exercises and playtime perform a very important role in your partner's life. Both give him a sense of fulfillment and allow you to keep your bond close. This activity is also a form of relaxation for the dog on his off days, as a game of golf or a tennis match may be for you. On these off days he learns he is among friends and does not need to prepare to combat someone who may hurt him. This time off will do wonders to lessen stress on your dog.

You are dedicated to your work with your dog and he is likewise dedicated to you. Follow the instruction given in this chapter and be aware of stress on your partner. It is something which you can understand and have the ability to do something about. Proper understanding and prevention can ensure a long comfortable working life for your partner. Should you have problems which are difficult to handle or understand, visit your veterinarian for assistance. He is always your closest and most reliable source of help.

Commands Given Under Stress Conditions

Case Study

At 03:28 hours on October 12, 1989 the Bellingham Washington Police Department responded to a call of a man with a gun. The suspect was seen walking down the street carrying an AR7 Survival rifle with collapsible stock in an upright position in front of him, in both hands. He was also wearing a backpack.

Officers responded to the call and confronted the suspect, who was unco-operative – he refused to put his weapon down when commanded to do so. A K9 officer was then asked to respond to the scene. The suspect continued to walk along the street as two officers, using available cover along the street, continued to challenge the suspect and order him to drop his weapon. The suspect responded only with threats to the officers and challenges for them to shoot him.

Officer David Doll responded to the call with his K9 Zeke. As he was coming on the scene a second K9 unit from the Whatcom County Sheriff's Office attended the scene and saw the suspect turn and run up an alley. The Deputy drove his patrol unit to a position which would enable him to cut off the suspect's flight. After stopping his vehicle, the suspect bolted in front of the unit as the Deputy drew his service weapon and challenged him.

Commands given to the dog under panic situations must be clear and concise, without confusion.

Officer Doll had pulled his K9 unit behind the Deputy's car and taken Zeke out of the car. As he approached on foot he saw the suspect lift his rifle towards the Deputy. At that point he commanded K9 Zeke to take down the suspect. As Zeke approached, the gunman turned his weapon towards the dog and fired one round into the dog's chest. He then lifted his weapon towards Officer Doll as the officer took evasive action and fired his service revolver at him. The suspect was killed from a gunshot wound to the chest. The dog stopped suddenly when struck by the bullet and sat down, although he showed no sign of being hit. The round which struck him was a .22 calibre bullet.

Subsequent training scenarios done with K9 Zeke after he recovered from his wounds showed the dog had a high propensity for tracking, yet he showed a form of avoidance when contacting real suspects. Tests on training tracks indicated he was not gun shy and had no hesitation about engaging decoys in training situations.

A study was done into the events leading up to the incident and it was learned that at the same time the suspect fired at the dog, Officer Doll yelled at the suspect. In seeing the suspect shoot his dog, his natural reaction was to scream "No!" Although it was not intended to be such, the screaming very likely seemed like a very forceful "No!" command to the dog. At the same time he received a very heavy correction, that being the bullet entering his chest. The gunshot could very likely have stopped the dog from continuing his attack – however, could it also have been the untimely command by the handler, unwittingly given, which caused the dog to cease his actions? There is no way to tell.

This case shows that under stress an officer may react in a way which will affect the dog's actions. Be aware of how your actions affect your K9 partner. Obviously, there is no way of knowing how we will react in all situations. However, we can learn a valuable lesson from Officer Doll's experience. Be aware your dog may react in a way you are not prepared for. He may act in a natural response to your verbal or physical communications, even though they are intended for the suspect or another officer. You must be alert to this when working your dog in a stressful situation and choose your verbal commands carefully.

Another aspect of commands under stress is the choice of many handlers to use German or Dutch commands when working their dogs. Officers who train their dogs in foreign languages often revert to English in an emergency. This causes confusion and raises serious questions as to whether the dog should be converted to English commands when imported from another country. It does not take long for them to learn new commands.

Under stress conditions many officers unintentionally use their natural language. Considering the types of situations we face, one must realistically consider the value of choosing one language over another.

4

4
The Basics of Survival

Mental And Physical Preparation

Mental preparation can provide an officer with confidence in his abilities to overcome the uncertainties and fears which often arise in serious and deadly confrontations. The ability to cope mentally with any serious incident will have a strong influence on physical survival.

Before you ever hit the streets you can prepare yourself mentally by building and maintaining an "I will get you, I will survive" attitude. A positive attitude will show, even to the suspect.

> Control your fear. Allow it to do its job, but manage its results.

Do not let fear control you. If you can control fear, you can control your situation.

If a deadly situation suddenly confronts you and puts you on the defensive, your mindset should be such that you take the offensive as soon as you can assess your situation. This sudden change of posture is obvious to your opponent, who will soon be on the defensive and more likely to give up the fight. An attitude which demonstrates confidence plus the effective application of your survival skills will have a strong psychological effect on your opponent.

In policing and particularly when working a dog in situations where you are not in control of what may occur on the track, always expect the unexpected. One of the idiosyncrasies of law enforcement is that things are often not as they appear. People are deceptive and often cunning. They can be extremely dangerous and intent on assaulting you while approaching you in a friendly manner. Do not take anything at face value until you have had a chance to assess your situation.

A major personality fault of police officers is their inability to admit they cannot do the job. A typical example of this is a K9 handler who is requested to do a door entry with a SWAT team, when he has never trained for such a situation. Rather than turn the assignment down and risk the criticism of his peers, the officer takes the risk, not even knowing himself how his dog is going to react to the situation when the action starts. Never take on a task you or your dog are not fully capable of handling. To do so is to put yourself, your dog and your fellow officers in jeopardy.

Just as mental preparation helps you to keep your confidence up during serious confrontations, physical fitness is also vital. Keeping yourself in good physical condition also helps you with your confidence level and plays a heavy role in your mental conditioning. Physical fitness reduces stress, builds stamina and gives you more confidence in yourself. This increased confidence in turn boosts mental awareness. It is not hard to see where both mental and physical preparedness becomes a cycle of support, one for the other.

You work high-risk times when assigned as a dog handler. Hours of darkness between 20:00 hours and 04:00 hours are the most frequent time for dog calls. As a K9 Officer you will also work most high-risk crimes, which will make you more prone to attack than most other officers. The way in which you approach your calls will often be a deciding factor in many incidents.

Case Study

On October 15, 1985 Deputy John McCroskey responded to a burglary at the W.F. West High School in Chehalis, Washington. Here is the story in his own words.

> "I responded to a request from Chehalis Police to assist them with a burglary. While en route I was told the suspect had broken out of the building and fled into a residential area. I pulled up and was contacted by a Chehalis officer who showed me where the suspect had last been seen. At this point a track was started with the dog off-line and we went into the neighborhood along a small creek. An escorting officer was with me when the track started. We crossed the creek and went through a couple of yards, crossing fences and streets. This continued for several blocks. Somewhere along the line I lost my backup man. While I was going over a fence I became tangled and was delayed for a few seconds. When I managed to get free I knew only the direction the dog had generally gone and I followed in that direction.
>
> A few moments later the officer in one of the containment cars saw a suspect cross the street in front of him and advised me. I went in that direction and then was told a citizen had advised there was a hurt dog in his back yard. When I got there I found my K9 Ward, obviously dead, laying under a roll of wire. When I looked at Ward there was a small thin line behind his shoulder which looked like a knife wound. Later that proved to be the case. Officer Bob Willey and K9 Cody from Centralia Washington were then called in to assist, which eventually resulted in the capture of the suspect.
>
> What I learned from this was that I was having so much fun chasing the crook that I was paying no attention to being careful. I was so sure what I was chasing was some 16-year-old kid who broke into the school to write 'screw you' on the blackboard and not a real bad guy.
>
> When I found Ward dead, next to a fence and in a corner where the suspect could hide and not be seen, I realized how foolish I had been. The suspect could not have known until the last second whether it was a police dog or a policeman closing in on him.
>
> If I had it to do over again, the only thing I could do different is apply tactics and give myself the edge. Nothing I could have done would have saved Ward,

although it would not have been easy to convince me of that at the time. I was pretty sure I had let Ward down. The morning after, when my wife asked me where Ward was and I told her he had died, she said she was glad that I was OK. At that moment I realized in all likelihood, Ward probably saved me or one of the other officers that night."

Deputy John McCroskey and K9 Ward. K9 Ward died as a result of stab wounds inflicted by the suspect he was pursuing.

The following is Officer Willey's account of the incident where he took over the track.

"At approximately 01:09 hours Chehalis Police called requesting Centralia's K9 unit to assist in a burglary in progress. While en route to the scene I was advised the county K9 Ward had been killed by the suspect with a single knife wound in the heart.

I arrived on the scene at around 01:13 hours and was shown the area where the suspect crossed Grandview street observed by Deputy Grover. K9 Cody was deployed and an off-line track was initiated with Officer Wiese as backup. The track traveled behind the house on the south side of Grandview and from there to a set of railroad tracks directly behind the house, turning south along the tracks. The dog indicated that the suspect had fled into a field and turned back toward town. While tracking through the field we were advised the suspect had been seen fleeing the area by containment officers. We broke off the track and responded to the new location, with the assistance of one of the containment patrol units. Cody was redeployed at the new location and immediately gave indications of hot scent. He tracked north towards 13th street, crossed the street, went through numerous yards, and continued in this manner past 15th street, where he entered another yard.

Officer Bob Willey and K9 Cody were the team who successfully captured the suspect who killed K9 Ward. The suspect was found in possession of a bayonet and a loaded derringer.

Cody was showing extreme indications of being very close to the suspect. We were attempting to move as carefully as possible to avoid another dog getting killed so I commanded Cody to go down each time he was about to go out of my sight, until I could catch up and look around the corner.

Cody finally exited into a yard on 16th street and indicated very strongly the suspect was close. Officer Wiese and myself watched as Cody overshot a small storage shed and then immediately turned around and indicated inside the shed. Fearing for the dog's safety, I ordered him out and with Officer Wiese as backup, I looked inside the shed. I could see the suspect huddled down in a corner with his back towards me. I ordered the suspect to come out. He stood up and, wrapping a dark-colored jacket under his arm, stepped over a piece of plywood and out the back side of the shed. I ordered the suspect to stop but he bolted and continued to run. I sent the dog after him as we rounded the front of the residence. Other containment cars were converging on the scene from various directions. Cody made contact with the suspect several times in the legs as he was running, finally knocking him down. Containment officers then jumped on the suspect and cuffed him.

"I then reentered the shed with the Chehalis officers, where I had first seen the suspect and found a small loaded derringer pistol and a bayonet hidden where the suspect had been when I had first spotted him."

Deputy McCroskey started the track as we all do . . . excited and anxious to catch the bad guy. In this case he started with a patrol officer for backup, but the officer had dropped out of the pursuit after a short time. When he got hung up on the fence he had no one there to assist him. This did two things. If the suspect had gone to ground nearby, it would have left him vulnerable to gunfire while going over the fence. Secondly, his dog had gotten out of his sight. By the time he realized he was going to be hung up too long to catch up to the dog, the dog was already out of sight and the officer was too late to command the dog to wait. Under the circumstances, even had the backup officer been there to assist the Deputy over the fences, enabling to keep up with his dog and even if McCroskey had been downing his dog before going around blind corners, he likely still would not have been able to prevent what occurred.

We can't put our dogs down at every turn, however we should always be prepared to expect the unexpected. A juvenile offender is just as capable of carrying a firearm as an adult. He may only be breaking into a school, but he may also be very capable of homicide.

The second K9 team on the scene was better prepared mentally on their arrival because they had received information that the previous police dog had been killed. Willey put his dog down at each blind corner and checked before allowing his partner to proceed. These precautions cannot always be practically implemented, however proper mental preparation to approach each situation with caution cannot be stressed enough. The backup officer for Willey stayed with him and covered him throughout the entire track. Should there have been an armed confrontation with the suspect, or had Willey needed cover or assistance clearing a fence, the backup man was there. Also note the suspect in this case wrapped a jacket around his arm in anticipation of another dog attack.

In preparing to start a track, be sure you have a backup officer you know you can depend on. While on the track, be certain you know where your backup is at all times. Do not allow your backup to return to his car until you are finished. Take someone who is physically capable of keeping up.

> Remember: It is your life on the line . . . you choose the backup, the backup doesn't choose you.

Tactical Preparation

The potential for high risk situations is becoming more common as society continues to deal with an increasing crime rate. As a dog handler, you will be at greater risk for lethal confrontations as a direct result of K9 applications. There are many tactics which can be used to help you survive such encounters.

These tactics include techniques with the dog, proper use of body armor and other protective measures. However, proper mental preparation, with follow up reactive training is the best defense in a dangerous situation.

Reaction Time

Reaction time in a confrontation is directly affected by mental preparation, readiness and willingness to respond to a threat. The *reaction cycle* begins with the officer's perception of a dangerous situation – recognizing a threat exists. Once the threat is acknowledged, a plan of action must be devised which then turns into physical actions. The officer draws his weapon, moves to a position of cover and returns fire if the situation warrants it. This reaction may take substantial time, depending on his ability to handle the situation.

Reaction time can be greatly reduced by mental preparation and field readiness. This readiness is obtained by mental conditioning along with appropriate training. Training for such situations should produce a pattern of reactions which become second nature. These reactions can be drawn upon in an emergency, as immediate action plans, because there is little or no time for planning when the threat occurs. The more the training is repeated, the faster the officer's reactions to a threat will be. Reaction times are reduced because the officer has already formulated and trained continuously regarding how to control the situation. The planning is already done to a large degree, and motor skills react automatically to the situation, without waiting for the officer to suddenly formulate a plan as to what he is going to do.

Training Exercises

When setting up training programs, officers must think about what options might be open to them on a track after an armed suspect. Training exercises can be set up in a manner which allows the officer to practice his plan of action for each scenario. These exercises can be set up using decoys armed with Simunition or Paintball type weapons to provide realistic simulations. Training should also involve live fire training on a bush trail ambush course with setup targets in obscure locations. The officers work the training scenarios until they are responding to each situation instinctively. This intuitive response is the result of automatic motorsensory response, building "muscle memory."

An immediate action plan becomes a vital part of any officer's survival. Training includes moving and using available proper application and control of the dog. Upon entering a situation where the dog is indicating he is close to the suspect, the officer has his weapon drawn and ready to use.

The barrel of the weapon is always pointed where the officer is looking. This reduces reaction time should he need to fire. If he has properly prepared himself in training, his assessment of the situation will be fast and reaction instinctive. In all situations, including training, he must keep moving and be aware of cover. Giving directions over the radio will help him become aware of his position at all times and teach him to direct backup officers into position when under stress.

The officer is conditioned to reload at the first break in the fight which offers a safe opportunity to freshen the weapon. He is trained not to wait until he is out of ammunition before loading a new clip or speedloader.

Failure Drills

Suspects are starting to wear body armor when going out to commit offenses. In response to this increasing phenomenon, law enforcement officers must adjust their training to include "failure drills." Training should include single, double and multiple suspects and failure drills to compensate for the likelihood of the suspect being equipped with concealable body armor.

Shooting drills of this nature include mental preparation and physical follow-up training. This conditions the officer to shoot two rounds at body mass and one round into the head of the suspect. When encountering two suspects, double-tap both and while still covering the second suspect, fire one round to the head. This "failure drill" routine is referred to as the "double back."

The officer's system of engagement depends on his proximity to each suspect, the type of firepower each carries and the perceived threat. If the suspects are close together, the potential for success may be greater if using a single tap. If they are separated, the officer needs to be sure of his shots as it will take him longer to get on target. In this case he would double-tap. In each instance, he must follow through with the failure drill to be sure the suspects have been neutralized if it appears they are still a potential threat.

Controlling Fear

In any situation, the officer must control his fear. If the officer can control his fear, he has already won half the battle. Motor skills will take over when he is adequately prepared. His concentration will be first on the most immediate threat, or the threat which has the most devastating firepower. Training and his hours of preparation will take over at that point and allow him to methodically deal with each threat.

All the while, the officer must be aware that things are often not as they appear. Although he may have only contacted one suspect while on the track with his dog, there may very likely be a second or even a third suspect in the vicinity. He cannot relax when the initial encounter is over. Vigilance must be kept until adequate backup arrives and the scene is secure.

The Aftermath

Unfortunately, it is becoming more frequent for officers in today's law enforcement to get involved in lethal confrontations. Situations all too frequently result in the death of a suspect, the officer, an innocent victim and even the dog. This is a difficult subject to approach as many officers have different viewpoints on deadly confrontations.

Deadly Force

When in a situation where you must use deadly force to protect yourself or another person from grievous bodily harm or death, you make a decision which affects you for the rest of your life.

> The decision to employ deadly force cannot be made only at the time of confrontation. You must mentally prepare to deal with the possibility you may have to use deadly force in the course of your career.

If you cannot prepare for that and prefer not to think about it, then you are a danger to yourself, your fellow officers and the citizens you protect.

At the time of confrontation you must make a split second judgment to shoot. In that tiny capsule of time you must decide whether it is legally appropriate under the circumstances and if there is any more reasonable means to protect yourself or someone else. You must judge the situation and determine if you can safely fire at the suspect without endangering bystanders. There is a lot of decision making taking place in the space of a split second, and the decision must be made. The time of the confrontation is not the time for you to start making a moral decision about whether or not you are capable of employing deadly force.

It is never an easy decision to make, however the morality of applying deadly force must be dealt with before you ever hit the streets as a police officer. Emotions that deal with morals can cause you to hesitate. The suspect can kill you or another innocent person before you can react if you are suddenly wrestling with your personal feelings on the use of deadly force.

Should you encounter a situation which requires you to take the life of another person in the course of your duties, be prepared for the aftermath. You will second guess yourself. Others will second guess you. Often you will feel remorse and guilt for what you have done. This is neither wrong or unnatural and you will need to talk about it.

Most officers feel a need to talk about it with someone and yet fellow officers are hesitant to bring the situation up, due to the sensitive nature of the subject. Do not be afraid to share your experience with those around you. If you need to talk to someone, approach a friend you can trust and just talk it out.

Nothing can change the events which have occurred, so do not try to do so by second guessing yourself. It can only lead to confusion and self-destruction. Time will heal: you must be able to hit the streets being fully capable of going into a similar situation without hesitation. If you are not prepared to do so, you are a danger to yourself and your fellow officers.

A K9 handler in particular has to keep in mind another aspect of mental preparation. Your dog is your partner. He will give you his loyalty and his love to the end. We all become attached to our dogs in a way many people do not understand. From the start of training a special bond is built between the dog and handler which is instrumental in the dog performing to the highest standard. That bond can only be built from a genuine love for the animal and a dedication to the training program with the dog.

The dog is your partner, friend and also a much loved companion at home with the family. Anything which occurs on the job resulting in the death of the dog not only affects the handler, but has a profound effect on his family as well.

If your dog is shot while actively in pursuit of a suspect, it does not justify your shooting the suspect unless your life is in immediate danger. You cannot let your emotions take over. In particular, if you see your dog go down, do not get distracted by the pain of seeing your partner hit. You must concentrate on the suspect in a detached and precise manner, or you will be putting yourself at extreme risk. Control your fear and emotions and you will come out a survivor.

5

5
Range Training for K9 Applications

Range Training for K9 Teams

Range training for dog handlers is essential to officer survival preparation. The K9 officer must prepare himself to react automatically in threatening situations. Through consistent training he learns to react to a threat with a preconceived plan which is carried out automatically when a threat occurs. This prevents confusion and shortens effective reaction time.

The training must extend to include the dog. On many occasions dogs did not perform for their handlers in dangerous situations, not because they were poorly trained or incapable of doing so, but because their training did not include conditioning for gunfire.

Agencies spend many hours on the range, training officers in firearms techniques. Only a small portion of training if any, includes the K9 officer with his dog.

> Range work should be a requirement of any dog team before hitting the streets and a part of any basic training program.

Adequate preparation will prevent confusion and better prepare the dog for deployment where control is required in gunfight situations.

In the past, officers have trained their dogs to respond to gunfire by automatically attacking the assailant. This is still a common practice in many agencies – the reasoning being, if the officer becomes involved in a firefight, the dog will react in a manner which becomes an immediate threat to the suspect, thus diverting attention from the officer. Should the officer be wounded and go down, the dog will respond even if the officer is unconscious.

With today's patrol procedures, this method of response to gunfire must be scrutinized. More and more often officers find themselves in situations involving felony car stops and circumstances which require a stealth approach. A dog that is high strung, barks constantly and is highly agitated is hard to control. For example, when the K9 unit is the primary take-down unit in a felony car stop situation, the dog handler must maintain control of the suspects in the vehicle until backup arrives. A barking dog makes the situation more confusing and as he becomes more agitated, the officer's concern is split between the suspects in the vehicle and the dog.

The same problem occurs when involved with an armed suspect who may be firing at the team. The officer may have excellent cover from which to return fire. A lunging dog on a lead, or a dog responding automatically to gunfire, can result in confusion, unnecessary injury, or the death of the dog.

Training on the range can begin with the dog on lead, doing obedience work from a distance while other officers are firing. This range work is started after the dog has a solid obedience foundation and should not be done with a green dog. It is difficult to control some dogs as many are very gunfire aggressive. However, by keeping the sessions quick and intense it will help to keep the dog occupied and his mind on the work at hand. During the obedience profiles the officer introduces methods for *shoot and move techniques*. These techniques are taught off the range initially and progress onto the firing range as the dog becomes more proficient.

Shoot and move is simply the process of engaging a target from a position of cover and then moving to a new position of cover as the need arises. This is important training for the dog, since he learns to be under maximum control when the tension is high. Such tactics can be used when an officer engages a suspect and needs to move his position. It may not be beneficial to send a dog on the attack under certain circumstances, and in such situations the officer and dog must work together as a team. This will prevent the dog from becoming a liability when gunfire erupts.

Prior to advancing to the firearms range for shoot and move exercises, the sequence should be run through without gunfire to familiarize the dog. Once the dog is proficient at the exercise, the next move is to implement the use of blanks into the exercise.

To begin, the dog is placed in a down position beside the officer. The officer fires a series of blank rounds from his duty weapon at a short distance and encourages the dog to stay calm. This distance is progressively shortened until the dog is confident with the handler firing blanks while directly beside him and even while kneeling over him. Using blanks eliminates the dangers of accidents when training with a fresh dog not accustomed to gunfire. The sequence:

1. Engage the target.
2. The officer commands the dog to stay while he moves to a new position.
3. The officer recalls the dog to the officer's position.
4. The officer fires again.

This sequence of events is illustrated in a series of five pictures on the following pages.

"Shoot and move" technique. This training sequence shows the officer already moved to a new position. The dog is recalled into a position of cover. At no time does the officer take his eyes off his target.

58   K9 Officer's Manual

The next step of training is to put more pressure on the dog by moving from the original position after firing. The sequence:

1. Once in a new position of cover, the officer engages the target before recalling the dog.
2. If the dog moves from his position he is corrected and taken back to his original spot.
3. When the officer successfully fires at the target and the dog has stayed in position, the officer recalls the dog and engages the target with gunfire again.

The training continues in a natural progression until the dog is controllable at all phases of shoot and move training. This exercise stresses control of the dog and teaches him to stay in position under gunfire conditions unless directed to move by the handler.

Once the dog is adequately under control, the training can progress to live *scenario training,* where the officer is involved in mock gunfights with decoys. The decoy engages the officer in a mock gunfight where the K9 team must move between breaks in the gunfire. The training is extended to include moving while the suspect is shooting in the officer's direction. The dog must learn to concentrate on the officer and is corrected if he breaks to attack when not directed. This control work is an extension of his obedience profiles.

When training has progressed to the degree where the team can deploy rapidly and efficiently under gunfire situations, it is time to include apprehension of the suspect by the dog. The training is intermingled to include situations where the dog is required to attack in some circumstances and not to attack in others. This will enhance the control aspect of the training so he only attacks as directed. This is referred to as "conflict training."

Training is extended to include take downs under heavy gunfire from both sides and to include a take down of the suspect while the officer is engaging other targets. Once the team becomes confident working these profiles, they can implement live fire training.

Building search showing improper positioning of the dog, causing him to be exposed to potential gunfire.

Building search technique showing proper cover and positioning of the dog.

Note how little of the officer and dog are exposed when properly positioned. The dog still has a good visual down the hallway. Depending on circumstances, he can be positioned fully behind the wall if desired to prevent any exposure.

Training Scenarios

Officers can engage in mock gunfights using blanks. These training exercises are critical as extensive range work will allow the dog to become accustomed to the content of the exercises. As the team progresses, live fire routines can be included in the programs. A K9 officer may be lucky enough never to have to use his weapon to protect himself, but if he ever does need it, he can have the confidence that his dog will react appropriately. To enter a real situation and find the dog is confused by all the gunfire will only increase the risks.

FATS Applications

Most officers in North America have at one time or another used or seen FATS. This technological advancement has been used in the past by patrol officers to hone their skills in decision making for potentially lethal situations.

Manufactured by Firearms Training Systems Incorporated of Norcross, Georgia, this system provides interactive training which puts the officer through a decision-making process in potentially lethal situations. The system projects a life-size image on a screen (controlled by a computerized video disc system) and the firearms instructor chooses a scenario and keys in the commands for the program to begin.

The officer is armed with the same duty weapon he would carry on the street, except it is equipped with a laser system detectable by the computer. As the program lifelike image is projected on the screen, the scenario begins. The officer reacts to the situation which unfolds before him as he would normally working the street.

Some scenarios are routine situations. Others escalate into a lethal confrontation. Should the officer be required to fire in defense of life, the weapon sends a laser impulse to the screen which is detected by the FATS system.

Accurate hits result in the suspect falling to the ground and the scenario ending. This is followed by a computerized evaluation of whether it was a good or bad decision, the reaction time of the officer and a playback which shows shot placement. Should the officer wound the suspect, the suspect may fall, but continue to return fire until neutralized by the officer. If the officer misses entirely, the suspect continues his lethal action until the scenario shows the officer has lost, or until the officer kills the suspect. All activity is recorded and available for playback and hardcopy printout. A video system records the officer's actions and decision-making process. This allows the instructor to go over the scenarios at later training sessions and work one on one with the officer's problems.

In experiments conducted at the Pierce County Sheriff's range in Washington State, officers were tested on the system with their K9 partners. This was to determine how the dog would react and how well the officer maintained control of his dog and returned effective fire if the dog did react. It became apparent the dogs visualized the subjects on the screen as being real. Most barked and became aggressive towards the subjects on the screen as the situation became more aggressive. The officers learned how to draw their weapon, make decisions and return fire while maintaining control of the dog. This exercise was an invaluable experience for the officer.

Further tests were conducted at an International Police K9 Conference held in Canada. Each dog team responded to scenarios selected as appropriate for canine work. Results showed the dogs responding very realistically to the images on the FATS screen. The FATS system enabled the officer to combine gunfire from his FATS weapon with a sequence of scenarios showing realistic threatening behavior by the onscreen perpetrator.

For animals in the early stages of their training, the FATS system can provide a chance for the instructor to reinforce appropriate behavior. The instructor or human partner can also observe and correct inappropriate actions. The FATS system may also be useful in making early selection or rejection decisions of potential candidates, thus saving the agency costly training time.

Some teams with fully-trained animals commented they had never been able to safely practice the combination of one handed shooting with a police dog actively lunging at a realistic threat. The FATS system can be used for inservice practice and training of K9 team judgment and tactics while providing a documented record of requalification.

Most agencies who use the FATS system already have the scenarios and weapons needed to evaluate this additional training application. As always, the ability to practice tactical and judgmental skills, in situations as close to reality as possible, can provide the officer and his canine partner the critical edge they need.

It is unlikely in most situations that the officer will be in a lethal confrontation where he will have to maintain control of his dog beside him. In most circumstances the dog will be released to attack and divert the suspect in order for the handler to obtain cover and return fire.

There are also circumstances which do not warrant the release of the dog, but where there is a need to return fire and maintain control of him. For example: a "man with a gun" call where the suspect is contained and the officer has good cover with plenty of backup when gunfire erupts. To release the dog in such a situation would almost certainly result in the suspect killing the dog. The officer might be required to return fire and maintain control of his dog at the same time. In such circumstances the officer needs to know how the dog is going to react and how it will affect him.

In the tests conducted at the Canadian seminar, left-handed officers faced with a lethal situation were caught off guard, as they were holding the leash in their left hand when they had to draw their weapon. Reactions were slow, as the officer had to quickly change hands with the lead and maintain control with his weak hand while drawing his weapon and returning fire. To this end it is better for the officer to be taught to work the dog on his right side, opposite the normal training routines for right-handed officers. A left-handed officer will feel more natural if his dog is worked from the right side.

In most cases the shot placement by handlers was erratic and spread upwards and to the right of the intended target. Most dogs were trained to attack immediately upon hearing gunfire. This caused some problems for handlers who were put in a position where the dog had to be controlled. A gunfire situation does not necessarily mean the dog should be sent automatically. This is a needless sacrifice of the dog.

Left-handed officers should consider training their dogs to perform on the right side, contrary to traditional training. This is more natural and frees up the weapon hand.

Other reactions from the dogs included the dog jumping up and attacking the handler's weapon, almost in frustration, others in confusion, showing a lack of adequate range work. In any case, the problems were discussed with each handler and then worked on once the officer attended the range. The FATS system was an integral part of working on specific control problems with some teams.

The following incident occurred in Delta, British Columbia and is a good example of a situation where the dog was not released under a gunfire situation. Under the circumstances it was wise judgment on the part of the officer. It should also be noted as a result of this incident, the officer changed his duty sidearm.

Case Study

Constable Gary West of the Delta Police Dept. attempted to check a suspicious vehicle in a remote area of the municipality. The vehicle was occupied by three juveniles, one of whom was heavily involved in white supremacy beliefs. When Cst. West tried to check the vehicle the driver initiated a pursuit which was short-lived – when the vehicle crashed into a fence. The officer stopped his patrol car in a position to block off the suspect vehicle. One of the occupants exited their car and aimed a shotgun directly over the hood of the patrol car at Cst. West. Before the suspect could pull the trigger, Cst. West put his car in reverse and backed out of the kill zone, calling for cover. The suspects immediately vaulted over a chain link fence and fled into a heavy bush area.

Corporal Tom Haworth, a dog handler with the Richmond, BC detachment of the RCMP at the time of the incident was called to help in locating the suspects. Haworth, with his police service dog "Smokey," proceeded to track the suspects, accompanied by Constable Garnett, a backup officer who was armed with a standard 13 cm (5 inch) .38 special revolver and a 12 gauge shotgun. At the time of the incident Haworth was carrying his 5 cm (2 inch) .38 special, common for dog handlers to carry at the time because of its small weight and size.

The area where the track began is a wide sand expanse near the end of an island. The end of the island is heavily forested, with some swamp. The track the team was working was confirmed by footprints in the sand, but they had to approach the woods in daylight conditions from a wide open area. This left the team fully exposed. The situation offered the three suspects an excellent point of observation, as well as a tactical advantage over the officers; however no resistance was met at this point. As the dog tracked into the wooded area, the officers saw the three suspects walking back towards them on a narrow gravel roadway. The lead suspect was carrying a sawed-off shotgun and a full belt of 12 gauge ammunition. When the suspects saw the dog team coming towards them, they turned and fled, with the armed suspect threatening to shoot the officers.

Under the circumstances, Corporal Haworth felt releasing the dog to attack would not be in order. The distance between the suspects and the officers was such that the armed offender could easily have turned and killed the dog before the dog could get close enough to neutralize him. It was more prudent under the circumstances not to release the dog. As the foot pursuit continued, the suspect turned to fire a shot at the pursuing officers. Haworth and the dog went left, while the backup officer went right, taking cover in ditches alongside the gravel road.

The suspect fired a shot and took cover in a wooded area about 30 metres (100 feet) ahead of the officers. Both officers proceeded forward toward the suspect's position. Haworth was able to see the armed suspect moving in the bush, but had lost sight of the other two offenders.

Gunshots were exchanged between the officers and the suspect. Haworth fired two rounds with his snub revolver at a distance of 12 metres (40 feet). One of the rounds narrowly missed the suspect's head, going by his ear. The suspect surrendered at this time. He was ordered to crawl to the officer's position of cover and Haworth covered the suspect while Garnett took custody, handcuffed and searched the suspect. The officers interviewed the suspect, who stated the other two had fled further and were not armed.

Garnett waited at the point of arrest for further backup to catch up and take custody, while Haworth continued to track. The track went through thick, heavy bush about 100 yards and continued into a swamp. The team continued roughly 90 metres (100 yards) further into the swamp in about 1 metre (3 feet) of water. The dog stayed in pursuit until locating the two offenders who were 9 metres (30 feet) apart in water up to their necks, trying to avoid detection. They were taken into custody without incident by three Delta Police Officers who had attended the area as containment members and were now in a position to cover Haworth.

6

6
Handler Control vs. Reasonable Force

Training Styles

Since the inception of European training methods in North America, law enforcement agencies have been able to benefit from various training styles learned overseas. A large portion of this training has been very beneficial to the quality of service dogs in the field. It has also been the cause of many differences between agencies with regards as to what the "best" training methods are. Whatever training method meets the agency's needs and is successful for the officer is obviously the method that should be used.

Training methods used by departments in Canada and the United States are progressive and diversified. There are some aspects of European training methods which are used effectively to improve the quality of street working dogs. There are, however, distinct differences in street applications of European dogs when used here in North America. These can promote liability problems as well as put the handler at unnecessary risk on the street.

One major difference to be considered before implementation is the use of the circle-and-bark as opposed to the bite-and-hold techniques of criminal apprehension. Both techniques have merit.

Reasonable Force (Circle and Bark)

The circle-and-bark method of apprehension (also referred to as minimum or reasonable force) was instrumental in Europe in saving the lives of service dogs used to patrol the borders. It became known by the underworld element who were illegally crossing borders that the dogs were trained to attack directly and hold on until called off by the officer. To defeat these dogs was relatively a simple matter of wearing protection from the bite on one arm. Once the dog attacked the protected arm, the suspect stabbed the dog to death. Since the dogs were working off-line, often far ahead and out of sight of the handlers, many dogs were lost. By the time the dog was located by the handler, he was dead and the suspect had escaped.

To combat this problem the authorities introduced a training style which would result in the dog harassing the suspect out of harm's distance by circling the suspect at a distance and barking to indicate his location to the handler. This prevented the suspect from stabbing the dog and indicated the location of the offender for the officer. Keep in mind these dogs would avoid contact with the suspect and were trained specifically to harass him. Under these circumstances this method is ideal for apprehension. It is used to combat a specific problem in countries where its application has successfully prevented further unnecessary loss of good service dogs.

This method of training was soon embraced by people who could see a possibility for marketing these reasonable-force dogs to North American law enforcement agencies. With continuing liability concerns in regards to the application of dogs in law enforcement, it is easy to see how this method of criminal apprehension could be seen as helping to reduce department liability.

The concept of a police dog trained to circle and bark as opposed to biting the suspect is easily marketed to any agency considering the implementation of a dog section but concerned with liability. Historically, most people who have promoted the circle-and-bark method of criminal apprehension are people involved in the Schutzhund methods of training.

Schutzhund Training

Schutzhund is a take-off of German Police training methods. It is the apprehension techniques used in Shutzhund training that cause a high degree of failure for dogs working the streets that are supposedly reasonable-force dogs. There is a distinct difference between properly trained German Police methods of reasonable force and the dogs marketed heavily in North America that are in fact Schutzhund-trained dogs.

Just as Schutzhund methods of tracking are not practical for police tracking situations, Schutzhund methods of apprehension are not practical for street applications. Schutzhund trainers and K9 suppliers commonly sell Schutzhund-based dogs to agencies under the guise that these dogs are reasonable-force dogs as they will not bite a suspect if the suspect stands still. There is little or no tolerance built into Schutzhund training for street applications however, and this gives rise to liability problems resulting from unnecessary bites by a so-called reasonable-force dog.

Handler Control

Handler control apprehension is used at present by most North American law enforcement agencies. Trainers who profess reasonable force to be superior to handler control techniques have given liability as the reason. It is a fallacy that liability originates from the bite. The bite is only the end result of an application of a dog in a given set of circumstances. Liability arises from improper application of the dog and lack of proper training or control of the dog. Failure to follow policy and procedure laid out by department policy, inadequate record keeping, and a host of other reasons can result in lawsuits. Liability can come in the form of a reasonable force dog, or a handler-control dog which is improperly applied. Improper or inadequate training in *either* style is potentially dangerous. Using either method, the dog must be able to react to situations appropriately.

Tim Tieken is a 23 year veteran of the Seattle Police K9 Unit. He is a highly respected trainer and has been with the K9 unit since 1974 who has held the training position there since 1980. He was one of the founders and past president of the Washington State Police Canine Association and has some valuable insight into bite-and-hold versus the reasonable force methods of training.

Tieken states:

> "In reality, the dog which is trained to bite and hold is only one member of a team. The other member is a trained officer who possesses judgment and controls the dog. That control is determined by department policy and existing law. The handler is able to read the behavior of the dog and is able to tell when he nears a suspect. If force is unwarranted the dog can be recalled at any time. Prior to applying the dog, a determination should be made as to whether a crime has in fact occurred, its severity, and the threat level of the suspect(s). Decisions can then be made as to how the dog will be applied.
>
> The philosophy of the bite-and-hold (handler control) method predicates itself upon handler safety issues and is not solely an attempt to preempt resistance or escape. The philosophy takes into account that the handler can make judgments and the dog can be called off. The level of ferocity of a bite and hold attack is generally misunderstood.
>
> I have deliberately stayed away from the circle-and-bark technique because I have seen its failures. The technique originates from the German dog sport known as Schutzhund. Schutzhund can be translated as protection dog. The dogs are judged in three categories: tracking, obedience and attack work.
>
> The dog is sent by the handler to search for a hidden man in an open area. When the dog finds the man he is supposed to bark and not bite unless the man moves. During trials and in training, the hidden man is a trained decoy with protective clothing. This man is highly skilled and is not afraid of the dog. He knows how and when to move, what eye contact to make or not to make and what sounds to make and how to make them to cause the dog to succeed or fail.
>
> All experienced decoys can sucker most any dog into an attack with near imperceptible motion, eye contact or sound. When demonstrated with a co-operative decoy, this exercise can be made to look quite impressive. However, on the street in the real world, its faults begin to show.
>
> Real suspects are not co-operative trained quarry. They are diverse. During the stress of a confrontation with a dog and officer, some will go into an uncontrollable panic, some become 'Chatty Cathies,' others will go into animated routines. All of these behaviors could evoke an attack from a circle-and-bark dog. I have had suspects try to climb on top of me to avoid my dog who was not biting them. By and large though, most suspects remain hidden and motionless in hope they will be passed over."

"Although most suspects do remain still, we do not know which ones will, or which ones are lying in ambush. A suspect hoping to be passed over, once discovered, can change tactics and shoot from concealment, under the cover of darkness. His opportunity to do so is enlarged if the dog allows movement. It does not take much movement to shoot a gun or swing a knife or club.

The canine handler is in a unique situation as he only responds to situations where a suspect has chosen to run and hide. These events are inherently high-risk and the canine handler is always the point man. As a matter of survival he must maintain any tactical advantage he has, although the suspect usually has all the advantages. He chooses the ground, the time and the movement. The handler has little advantage, only his dog's nose and teeth. A dog that doesn't bark can often make contact before the suspect can react. (The severity of the resulting damage is usually determined by the suspect's choice to fight or surrender.) As soon as the handler can determine the suspect is free of weapons, the dog can release the suspect. This is a far more humane method than allowing the fights and shootings which occur without the use of dogs.

I have spoken to German, Canadian, Norwegian, English and American trainers and handlers who operate under the guise of circle and bark, but will admit in trusted company circle-and-bark has a high degree of failure. When asked why they continue with it, they explain it would not be politically sound as their program was originally touted up as circle and bark to make it palatable to citizens or their administrators. This is deceptive and flies in the face of valid officer safety concerns. It does not take into consideration that a low bite ratio can be maintained on bite-and-hold dogs.

I have trained dogs for the revere and know that very few dogs can be trusted, and that even the more trustworthy dogs still have the intellect and judgment of a dog. I would rather place my trust in a trained handler who possesses the capacity to respond to the fact pattern he is presented with. To him, I can dictate guidelines and mandates which will allow him to be efficient and at the same time minimize the use of force.

In regards to litigation, in Pierce County Washington, litigation was recently completed on a case (Champney vs. Pierce County Sheriff Office). The court found in favor of the officer and in a countersuit the officer was awarded a $3000.00 judgment. At trial, a pivotal issue was bite-and-hold, as applied in this case, as opposed to the circle-and-bark method, which was unsuccessfully put forward by its proponents.

The U.S. Court of Appeals Sixth Circuit in a 1988 case (Estate of Daniel Briggs vs. Ronnie Barnes, an individual and employee of the Metropolitan Government of Nashville and Davidson County, Tennessee) found in favor of the officer. The decision is flush with logic supporting the use of force consistent in the policies and procedures of most police agencies using bite-and-hold dogs.

Litigation and liability are ever present factors. Our policies and procedures are the best defense. Each case will be judged upon its own merits, comparing the facts against a standard. If our standard is kept high, we may lose a case due to aberrant actions of an individual, or unavoidable circumstances, but we will not be shown negligent. Case law supports our present policies and application."

This statement provides strong arguments regarding handler-control training. The decision to apply the dog is multifaceted. The decision as to how the dog is to be applied must be left up to the handler, not the dog.

Application Results

Canada and the United States both have seen a dramatic increase in the use of firearms in the commission of offenses. There has also been a substantial increase in the number of young offenders carrying guns. A method of K9 application which is ideal for European situations does not mean it is ideal for North American problems. Note the keyword here is *application* as opposed to training.

The use of circle-and-bark dogs has resulted in the deaths of police dogs and possibly one officer in the United States. In each situation, the dog was trained as a reasonable-force dog, and each dog was killed when he was used to take down an armed suspect. In every case the offenders reacted in a cautious manner, which enabled them to bring a weapon into play. In one case the dog was sent to make an apprehension and when the dog failed to perform as directed, the handler left his position of cover to redirect the dog. The officer was shot to death.

In each case, the dog's basis of training was circle-and-bark, and each had been converted to police standards for street applications. However, in each case when tensions were high, every dog hesitated even though they were directed to attack. Most of the dogs involved had a method of training heavily based on Schutzhund sport training methods. This basis is one of the key problems, depending on the level the dog is at before it is converted and oriented to police training.

A well-trained service dog can be recalled at any point from the attack. Control of the dog through voice command permits the officer to call the dog off before or after the apprehension, as the situation warrants. Once the dog is called off, he is positioned where he can safely watch the suspect while the officer approaches and secures him. Total control is with the officer. This is termed "handler control."

If the suspect is intoxicated and unstable on his feet, or if he is loud and abusive, the dog is close enough to be of instant assistance to the officer if needed. However, he is also far enough away and conditioned in such a manner that he will tolerate such movement and actions by the suspect. This prevents the officer being concerned about the dog unnecessarily biting at his own discretion.

A reasonable-force dog is trained to attack when it perceives the suspect as aggressive, or as moving to escape. It takes many hours of training with a professional quarry to keep the dog "clean," and there is very little tolerance level in such a dog. When he locates a suspect and the suspect stumbles or moves accidentally, there is a high likelihood of an unwarranted bite. In such cases, it is only a matter of time before a good attorney has the case in civil court. It is hard to justify a training method where the dog makes the judgment as to the amount of force deemed necessary.

Officer safety techniques relating to reasonable-force dogs are tactically unsound in the way they are instructed by some agencies. Tactics used with handler-control dogs will not apply in some cases with reasonable-force dogs. It is important for the tactics of the officer to change along with the training style.

A reasonable-force trainer recently advised that his officers are trained to approach from a different direction than that of the dog. They are taught to approach cautiously, in a manner which allows them to observe the action from a different angle before approaching further. In the meantime the dog is up next to the suspect barking. This may not be feasible in most circumstances unless the dog is off-line and well ahead of the officer when the apprehension is made. While triangulating to a suspect is a preferred method of approach in any situation, it is not practical in many cases. When asked about the common use of firearms and the danger to the dog, the trainer stated it was an accepted risk using this type of application, but the dog would attack if a weapon was brought into play. Unfortunately experience has proven otherwise, resulting in traumatic loss of life – the major reason being that most of the dogs trained in reasonable force have not been conditioned into police-oriented reasonable-force methods, but in most cases are heavily Schutzhund- oriented.

In Yavapai County, Arizona, officers were called to a campus in response to a man with a gun. The suspect was a student who was unstable and armed with a shotgun and a .45 automatic handgun. By the time officers arrived at the scene, the suspect had shot one person critically and seriously wounded two others.

The dog handler exited his car in the area and could hear a disturbance not far from his location. The dog, which was close to retirement, was a reasonable-force dog. When the officer came around a building he could see the suspect, with a friend, standing in the middle of a parking lot. Two patrol cars were parked at the end of the lot with their headlights and spotlights on the suspect. As they got into position, the friend of the suspect suddenly ran off as the suspect became more aggressive towards the officers. At the same time, the officer sent his dog on the suspect. At the time, the location of the suspect was such that the officer was able to get close by staying in the shadows. There was no available cover for him. When the dog was released, he immediately pursued the friend of the suspect who was fleeing. The dog was called off and redirected towards the suspect by the handler. As he redirected the dog, the officer realized he was at a point of no return. There was no way he would be able to get back to cover before the suspect could take action. The dog went after the suspect and performed a revere on the suspect. The suspect kept turning and hitting the dog with the shotgun, but the dog never attacked.

The suspect pulled the trigger on the shotgun and the firing pin fell on an empty chamber. The suspect dropped the weapon and the dog stood over the shotgun watching the suspect. The handler moved in, thinking it was all over, when the suspect reached into his waistband, drew a .45 automatic and pointed it at the officer. The K9 officer fired two rounds, striking the suspect, however the suspect continued to point the weapon. The officer fired a third round, killing him.

In this case the family of the suspect involved initiated what turned out to be an unsuccessful lawsuit against the officer. One of the reasons stated was the failure of the dog to apprehend the suspect. Their position was that if the dog succesfully made the apprehension, the officers might not have had to take the young man's life. The officer was cleared of any wrong doing.

It is a matter of personal survival that police dogs be trained to take down a seemingly passive suspect. If an agency uses reasonable force dogs, they need to be aware of its possible ramifications and limitations. Independent studies by agencies considering changing their programs from handler control to a reasonable force style of training have concluded there is more danger to the officer and the dog with the latter.

There are agencies which have taken the reasonable force routines and have properly applied them within their agencies. The dogs used by these agencies are not Schutzhund degree dogs sold as police dogs. They are dogs which have been purchased, raised and trained by police officers who are active K9 officers. The methods used are those methods instructed in the German police methods of reasonable force.

Alaska has legislated the use of reasonable-force dogs within the State. Anchorage Police K9 Officer Garry Gilliam has implemented a program which has been very successful in the application of reasonable-force dogs. The Denver Police K9 Unit under Terry Rogers has also implemented a proper reasonable force program based on law enforcement concepts as opposed to Schutzhund ideals. The training provided uses a progressive concept which succesfully combines the best of both worlds for these agencies. It has not been done without many hours of consistent work and training. Both trainers make it clear that they train effectively because they use police methods to accomplish their goals and make no attempt to convert a dog which has been worked on extensively to obtain Schutzhund degrees.

If an agency chooses or is required to train in the reasonable-force methods it is important they implement the program properly. Failure to do so will put the personal safety of officers and dogs at risk. Reasonable-force training programs are usually implemented to counter liability concerns. If training is not adjusted, the dog handler takes on increased risks from an officer safety point of view. If not properly trained and applied, a reasonable-force dog may even increase an agency's liabilities. This has proven to be the case by past experience.

The use of reasonable-force dogs has become popular with some administrations because of lawsuits generated by improperly trained handler-control dogs, or misapplication of a dog which has injured a person without just cause. The misconception is that such incidents are the fault of the dog and not the handler's application of the dog or lack of proper training. This causes the uninformed to call for methods of training and deployment that become more restrictive in the belief that it will solve the problems.

Switching to reasonable-force applications will not solve the problems. Groups such as the ACLU who advocate moving police dogs into reasonable-force training will only cause more difficulties for smaller agencies who cannot afford training budgets to accommodate the costs of reasonable force training methods. The end result will be the same . . . reasonable-force dog teams as well as bite and hold dog teams that deploy improperly or without just cause will still result in unwarranted injuries to suspects or citizens.

Summary

Handler-control training methods are presently under fire, largely due to the misinformation being disseminated about their techniques. It is the responsibility of officers who use bite-and-hold applications to keep the work standards high and K9 applications within the use of force continuum. In showing restraint and good judgment, you demonstrate your professionalism and protect the higher degree of officer safety methods that handler-control techniques provide.

It is the responsibility of all dog handlers regardless of the apprehension methods they deploy, to support each other in their applications. My experience has shown me that there is in fact very little difference between the two methods. The training for both techniques is virtually parallel with the exception of the final apprehension.

7

7
Tracking

Tracking Applications

Criminal Psychological Aspects

When a K9 officer pursues a fleeing suspect, there are several factors which come into play. Wind scatters the scent while extreme temperatures can freeze or evaporate it. Moderate to heavy rains can wash it away. Vehicular and pedestrian traffic also disturb the surface scent. Any of these factors alone, or in combination can defeat the dog. Time delays magnify these problems.

In the mid 1980s, the Calgary City Police dog section obtained information from the University of Alberta to learn how the brain performs under certain situations. The patterns of behavior were compared to successful tracks completed by members of the police dog section. The information revealed surprisingly consistent behavior between suspects. This information has proved to be effective when applied by dog handlers working tracks.

When the dog loses a track and is unable to recover and continue, the officer can bring his skills into play as a personal tracker. Mantracking, combined with criminal psychological profiles of fleeing suspects, can often result in a recovery of the track for the dog. Patrol officers have also used the same skills to recover evidence when there is no dog team available. These techniques have also been effective in locating suspects who have fled the scene of a crime.

Passive and Active Tracks

Tracks left by individuals are categorized into two basic groups, passive tracks and active tracks.

Passive Tracks and Officer Safety

Passive tracks are those tracks left by people who are not in any rush or panic, and under little or no pressure to avoid detection. This includes lost persons, elderly people who walk away from homes and even criminals who do not feel pressured by their circumstances. When in pursuit of a suspect who is not excreting a lot of scent the dog will frequently work the track giving indications that the trail is old. This can be deceptive and potentially dangerous.

Information provided by Dayle Meyers, a bloodhound handler from California, indicates that I.V. drug users frequently fall into the category of a passive track. He states that the suspect's body does not pump large amounts of adrenalin because he is high and not exhibiting fear. Even as the dog closes in on the suspect, he may not give the officer his usual indications of the suspect being in close proximity. The lack of usual indications by the dog may put the officer on top of the suspect without any warning. This is a potentially dangerous situation should the offender be armed. The handler must be alert to the problems a passive track can cause.

Active Tracks

The active track is what we deal with the most. As a result, we know the suspect we are after is under pressure to avoid apprehension. The person may or may not know he is being pursued, however, due to the nature of the crime he is intent on putting as much possible ground between him and the crime scene.

When attending the crime scene, you need to obtain as much intelligence as you can on your suspect: the point where he was last seen, or most likely to have been; if a robbery, what type of weapon he produced – if it's a gun, get some idea as to what calibre of weapon. This all helps in your mental preparation. Obtain description details of the suspect, including clothing. Physical features are most important. Keep in mind that many suspects discard clothing or change at a predetermined location to assist in masking their flight.

If possible, determine if there is more than one suspect. I also like to find out if the person appears to have been drinking. If so, is he heavily intoxicated? I have had tracks end rather abruptly when the dog located the suspect within a few hundred yards of the crime scene because he was too drunk to formulate a plan of escape. They simply go to ground and hide rather than continuing their flight.

Eluding Arrest

Suspects attempting to elude arrest show surprisingly similar manoeuvres when leaving crime scenes. The most common habits which occur are:

1. A suspect exiting a doorway will usually turn to the latch side of the door.
2. When crossing from a street to an alley, or vice versa, he will use the right side of a house, even if the left side has a walkway and the right side is obstructed by a high fence.
3. In running down an alley or street, the suspect will use the right side.
4. If he can be forced by your containment to use left turns, he will panic and go to ground, which allows the handler a better possibility for capture.
5. Normally the suspect will only employ left turns to avoid immediate capture, or to gain some distant objective which cannot be reached by using right turns. In most cases, the suspect's first turn will be to the left, followed by a series of consecutive rights.

6. Evidence discarded or thrown by the suspect is normally tossed on the right side of the track.

7. Two or more suspects running together will go to ground faster than a person traveling alone. Should one suspect be apprehended, the second suspect will often stay close to the scene. At times this suspect will make a wide circle to the right to return to the scene to see what is happening with his partner. Once his partner is removed from the scene, the second subject will resume his flight. Suspects apprehended on the scene by patrol or by police dogs should not be removed from the scene. Keep arrested suspects secured within sight of the surrounding area. Associates are curious as to their companions' situation and will often stay close by to see what is happening to their friends. This curiosity often leads to their own demise.

8. Eighty percent of all urban tracks terminate within four blocks.

If applied effectively this information can help in relocating tracks the dog has momentarily lost. All too often new dog handlers depend entirely on their dog to track and locate the suspect, but too much dependence on the dog will often lead to failure where success could have developed.

Tracking Issues

Case Study

On an early fall morning, Langley RCMP Detachment in British Columbia was summoned by a woman claiming a man had just broken into her house and was in the kitchen. While she was talking to the emergency operator, the dispatcher sent patrol members to the scene. Corporal Haworth and police service dog Smokey responded to the call to back up the first member on the scene.

The complainant stated the suspect's first name over the phone and said he was approaching her. She was pleading for help. At this point the phone went dead.

A few minutes passed before the investigating officer and Corporal Haworth arrived. They immediately checked the house, finding the rear door ajar, but no sound of anyone inside. The following is Corporal Haworth's report on how he handled the incident.

> "I immediately entered the house calling for the complainant but received no reply. Police dog Smokey, after entering the kitchen area, directed his attention down the main hall of the house. I could see a woman lying on the bedroom floor, obviously seriously injured. Each room leading down the hall was carefully cleared as we made our way towards the woman. It was obvious she had been shot or stabbed several times. I completed clearing the house for any possible suspects and took up a search of the exterior of the residence in search of the suspect.

"The residence was on a large ten acre lot surrounded by similar residences. Exiting at the rear sliding door, Smokey immediately cast around to locate any track leaving the area. Almost immediately he indicated a large bush area and attempted to enter, but it was impossible to do so, even for the dog, as the vines were heavily entwined and overgrown. I made a mental note of the indication by the dog and redeployed him to cast around again.

As the dog approached the front door in search of a track, he located one leaving from the front door area. The track was obviously very fresh, as indicated by the dog, and led directly east towards the main road.

Pursuit was taken up carefully, as it was not known what the suspect had for a weapon. The night was clear and the moon was full, which put the advantage in the suspect's favor for visibility. As the track was leading us on a slow upward incline, our movements would easily be seen or heard by the suspect.

Smokey led us along the track for approximately one quarter of a mile. The track proceeded to a residence, across a gravel walkway and through a patio area to the north- east side of the house. At this point Smokey indicated on a window of the house and attempted to enter it. The window was closed at the time and I attempted to have Smokey continue the track, however, all attempts failed as he insisted the track ended at this window.

We secured the residence by taking up positions where both the front of the residence and the suspect window could be observed, while my backup officers took up a position of cover to the rear and opposite side of the house. With the residence secured, more backup was called and the investigating members attended.

The occupants of the residence were co-operative and assisted the members immediately. The room where Smokey had indicated the suspect was inspected and found to contain a young male suspect as well as evidence confirming his involvement in the offense."

Analysis

Upon successful completion of the arrest, Corporal Haworth returned to the crime scene and directed his dog to search the area of his first strong indication in the heavy bush. Approximately 9 metres (30 feet) into the bush, Smokey located the source of the odor . . . a kitchen knife covered in blood. The evidence was seized and turned over to investigating officers. Murder charges resulted.

This case is a textbook example of proper deployment of manpower and proper approach of a crime scene. Although the suspect had in fact left the scene, there was a high likelihood he could have still been within the residence and so pose a danger to attending officers. Corporal Haworth entered the residence with his dog and a backup officer, and although it became apparent the victim was badly wounded, they ensured they properly cleared the residence before proceeding. Too many officers would have immediately put themselves at risk by exposing themselves to give aid to the victim. Remember, you cannot be of assistance if you are injured or killed while trying to get to a victim. Do not let your personal feelings get in the way of your safety or common sense.

In cases such as this, it is easy for your dog to miss a suspect who may be hiding within the building, even though he is an excellent building searcher. In a building where a large quantity of blood has been spilled, you must not depend on your dog's indications to locate a suspect.

Blood, the Strongest Source Of Human Odor

Blood is the strongest source of human odor. Just as it is difficult for a dog to locate a large cache of drugs in a room, so it is with suspects in a blood soaked area. The scent is so strong it permeates the room and in some cases, the entire building, with strong human odor. External odor given off by a suspect will not be as strong and therefore, difficult if not impossible for the dog to work with. You must be sure to clear every possible location for suspects as carefully as you would without a dog.

Conversely, a suspect who is bleeding or covered in blood and who has left the crime scene, will give off a strong odor and be easier for the dog to track. For example, a suspect who has cut himself during a burglary and then left the scene may be able to be tracked through heavier than normal contamination due to the strong source of odor.

A suspect's genetic makeup determines his distinctive odor. Although there are numerous other factors which compose body odor, the genetic imprint cannot be changed. It is distinctive to that individual. A blood trail is very strong in odor and detected easier and with more accuracy by the dog, often with extended time delays and heavy contamination.

In Corporal Haworth's statement, he explains how his dog was giving strong indications in a heavy bush area which was obviously too thick for human passage. He made a mental note of the location and returned later to search the area again, resulting in the recovery of the murder weapon. Too often we take what is obvious to the dog and work on that aspect of a crime scene. How many officers would have continued working the dog until locating the weapon before leaving the location and trying to locate a track leaving the area? You are also a team member and it is your abilities as an investigator and skills as a dog handler which make the difference.

There will be times when a dog indicates something which is not immediately obvious. If unable to immediately find what has piqued his interest, continue the track and make a mental note to return and search the area later. After exhausting all possibilities for completing the initial track, the dog can be redeployed to area search where he was showing interest.

In Corporal Haworth's statement it is apparent he was concerned about his concealment and the amount of noise he was making. He states his concern about a quiet night with a full moon. He had a backup officer with him at the time and worked the track efficiently until locating the probable location of the suspect.

Ask yourself how you and your backup officer would have handled such a situation. For example, would your backup officer have the windows on the residence covered, had the suspect suddenly fired at the handler when his dog reached the base of the window? It is a likely place of concealment for a suspect and in fact was where the suspect was found. Many times I have done similar types of tracks after suspects along the side of a residence and never thought about the windows I was passing by. This is an example of the type of awareness you and your backup team should have. Keep in mind, things very often are not as they appear.

The following circumstances occurred in Washington State. The situation is one of the best examples of the importance of having backup officers who are aware of the handlers needs.

A suspect facing this situation is very unlikely to confront the officers and will invariably shoot at the dog first. In this scenario he has four direct problems to deal with.

Case Study

Deputy Kevin O'Shaugnessy of the King County Sheriff Office responded to a call to track a robbery suspect armed with a .357 magnum revolver. At the start of the track the officer was accompanied by two backup officers who were both armed with shotguns. During the track both backup officers got separated from the dog handler. Deputy O'Shaugnessy was subsequently on his own when his service dog, K9 Jake, encountered the suspect. The suspect first engaged the dog, shooting the dog in the head and chest, and then also managed to shoot the officer twice. In the subsequent firefight the suspect was shot by Deputy O'Shaugnessy and successfully apprehended. The dog survived the wounds he sustained and eventually went back to work on the street. In this case several circumstances occurred. First, the officer was alone when the confrontation occurred. The suspect fired on the dog first. The dog is the immediate threat to the suspect.

Investigation revealed the suspect had carefully selected a location to confront police, one which would afford him cover and leave the officer in the open. This is a favorite strategy of suspects who are setting up for ambush. The suspect forces the officer into the open while he waits in bush under cover.

> In all cases, the suspect knows the point where confrontation will take place.

He chooses where the fight will occur. He prepares himself and waits. He has a plan. You must also have a plan which is flexible enough and effective enough to counteract his attack. Suspects often use open areas to circle back to a vehicle or get behind you. However, if a suspect is not familiar with the area and feels disoriented, he will likely go to ground.

Position the dog so the suspect's focus is on the dog, not on your approach.

We all talk about the need to have backup officers with us on tracks. Yet for one reason or another we all end up going on tracks after suspects on our own, probably more often than not. We must be especially cautious and prepared to handle situations on our own. When the worst situation which can occur does occur, it is always worse when we are alone.

Approaching Apprehended Suspects

When the dog apprehends a suspect on a track, be alert to the surroundings as you prepare to make an arrest. When after a suspect believed to be armed it is best to leave the dog on the suspect until his hands are clearly visible to you and you have done a quick search of the suspect's waistband. In some cases it might be preferable to handcuff the suspect before calling off the dog.

In most cases the dog will be called off and directed into a position to watch the suspect. It is best to approach the suspect by a system of triangulation; that is, the dog is to one side of the suspect with the suspect facing the dog, while the officer approaches from behind the suspect at a different angle. The suspect's attention is focused on the dog and affords the safest opportunity for the officer's final approach. Handcuff the suspect and do a complete physical search before proceeding any further.

When working with multiple backups triangulation comes easy. The handler can concentrate on working the dog and keeping an eye on the surrounding area while the backup officers complete the arrest.

8

8
Tracking On-line vs. Off-line

Methods of Tracking

From a tactical point of view, both on-line and off-line methods of tracking have merit. There is also a negative side to both applications. I have trained extensively in each method and still train officers in both styles, according to what their individual preference is. I have come to the conclusion that on-line tracking is the best producer for me in my area and as a result, I use an on-line method of tracking when working the street.

I originally trained using a harness and line until I had an opportunity to participate in a training program where I worked entirely off-line. I worked off-line for a year after coming back from the program and was relatively successful with my new dog. It was after a discussion with a colleague who critiqued an off-line application, that I decided to go back to on-line tracking.

Case Study

This colleague observed my dog while we were tracking a burglary suspect using an off-line method. I was called to the scene of a residential burglary and had started the dog on the track. He immediately went in pursuit of the suspect and located a jacket discarded on the track. We soon lost the track on a road surface and were unable to relocate it, and subsequently the search was called off.

My colleague later advised me that he watched how my dog was trailing the suspect, and he was not consistent in his work. The dog tracked so fast I would fall behind and so he kept breaking his concentration on the track to stop and wait for me. The dog was also losing the track whenever the scent drifted or was dispersed from the air. That is, if the dog could not trail scent the suspect, he would quit rather than put his nose down to the ground to locate the ground scent. This meant that time delays could diminish my chances for the success of a track very easily.

I decided to go back to on-line tracking and work harder with the dog on the nose down tracking as opposed to the trailing method. This resulted in a dramatic increase in my capture rate. My dog was more methodical on the track and could concentrate fully on hard surface work. He was not so quick to give up if the trailing or tunnel scent was gone, as he would put his nose to the ground and work on the contact scent. As a result, I have stayed with the on-line method of tracking.

This is not to say I never freetrack, or that off-line tracking is not a proper application. Quite the contrary. In certain areas one method will be better than the other. You must consider your working conditions and decide on what method will work best for you.

On-line Applications

On-line tracking, if properly applied, is beneficial as it allows you total control of the dog. The dog has less of a tendency to overshoot the turns in a track. This reduces the chance your dog will pull you past a suspect who has gone to ground. Even though the dog uses airborne scent to trail the suspect, he works the scent on the ground as well. When the dog comes to corner, he will find it far easier than a dog which is following trail scent on the run.

Scent has a tendency to drift and blow in wide patterns off the original track. Trailing dogs will follow the airborne scent and often overshoot the corner of the track. They will often vary so far it is sometimes difficult to get back on track if there is a lot of drifted scent in the area. The on-line dog will have more of a tendency to find the corner and make the turn in the proper location.

An on-line tracking dog is not expected to track footprint to footprint as does a Schutzhund trained dog. The method is too slow for street level work. The dog will not lift his head and give you an indication as quickly as a dog that takes advantage of both ground and airborne scent.

> You want your dog to use the trailing scent as well as the contact scent.

This enables him to use his natural speed and you to take advantage of his early indications you are closing on a suspect.

Officers using trailing dogs must exercise more caution because of their tendencies to overshoot the scent.

From the viewpoint of officer safety, there are a few aspects of on-line tracking which are particularly beneficial. A seasoned dog handler can "read" his dog in total darkness by the way the dog leans into the harness and the type of pull on the tracking line. By working on-line, the officer maintains contact with the dog in darkness, without having to use his flashlight. This prevents him from having to expose his position.

A dog working on-line will work slower than a free-tracking dog and will not likely run past a suspect's location. For example, suppose you are after an armed robbery suspect who has fled into a back alley and is running along the right side of the alley northbound. The wind is from the south.

He proceeds down the alley and near the end of it, finds a small clearing covered in dense brush. You get to the scene and put your dog on the track. An off-line tracker will track the suspect at a run with the officer following behind. The dog is working only the airborne scent. From the point where the suspect has turned off to the right there is a lot of scent still drifting in a northerly direction.

The dog will follow the strong airborne scent and likely run past the point where the suspect turned in. It is not unusual for the dog to trail 30 metres (100 feet) past a turn. If you are running behind your dog and are within 15 metres (50 feet) of him, there is a likelihood of you running right by the suspect, exposing yourself to danger. What saves most situations is that the dog has usually figured out the corner and is on top of it before we get that close.

If working on-line, your dog is more likely to pick up the corner and give you a more accurate indication of the turn. If you and your dog are on the scene together, there is less likelihood the suspect will want to engage you both at the same time. If he does, the dog will be his first priority.

The on-line method also gives you constant continuity for court. You never lose sight of your dog and can testify that the dog tracked consistently on the track he started, to its completion. The major disadvantage of on-line work is you are only 10 metres (30 feet) behind your dog. Once you start to get close-in indications from your dog, you know you are probably within shooting range of your suspect. This can leave you exposed to the suspect as your dog closes in for the final apprehension. In such cases where you are in pursuit of an armed suspect, release your dog to work off-line. Draw your weapon and get to cover. Allow your dog to close in on the suspect while you cover him from a protected position.

Off-line Applications

Once you try off-line tracking, it is hard to switch back to on-line work. There is something about off-line tracking which is very addictive. I know I had a difficult time deciding to switch back to on-line work after having experience off-line tracking.

Off-line work can be effective in rural, bush and suburban areas where the conditions are conducive to trail scenting work. A good free tracker can rapidly close the gap on a fleeing suspect if conditions are such that the suspect's tunnel scent is still available to the dog. This is where these dogs excel. While the speed of the dog is an advantage in the pursuit of suspects, it can also be a disadvantage as you cannot keep up with your dog. Off-line tracking dogs often get out of sight of the handler. The continuity of the track can come into question if it is proven in court your dog was not always within your sight.

Working off-line does offer an advantage in officer safety as the dog is usually far ahead of the officer. He contacts the suspect before the officer comes into range of potential gunfire.

A technique beneficial when in pursuit of fleeing suspects. This routine helps you to close the gap quicker, with less danger of injury to the dog.

Reflective Harness

When working a dog off-line make use of a reflective harness equipped with a strobe light. The system allows me to locate my dog with a sweep of a flashlight if necessary. When the strobe light is in operation, the officer knows where the dog is at all times and does not have to expose his location to the suspect by using a flashlight. In experiments with the strobe-equipped harness, the suspect cannot pinpoint the dog. The dog moves 6 to 15 metres (20 to 50 feet) between flashes and often in opposite directions when working the scent cone. Training experiments conclude that strobe lights confuse decoys, to the ultimate benefit of the dog and officer. The suspect sees the dog in one direction and by the time the strobe flashes again the dog is on top of him, often approaching from a different angle.

A reflective off-line tracking harness may be beneficial during searches or lengthy tracks, depending on circumstances.

When using a strobe-equipped harness the suspect's attention is focused entirely on the light source. The suspect momentarily forgets about the officer while unsuccessfully trying to pinpoint the dog. This system is a valuable psychological advantage. It was described to me by one burglary suspect my dog apprehended: "It's like listening to the theme song from Jaws as you watch the shark closing in on you." This is a natural reaction and beneficial for the safety of the officer as the suspect's entire focus of attention is on the dog.

One major disadvantage of working off-line is the lack of control on the dog and the cover the officer can provide him. Many free tracking dogs have been struck down and killed by passing motorists. The dogs suddenly bolt into traffic while pursuing a suspect before the officers can react and recall them. The aspect of covering the dog comes into debate and it is something each officer or agency has to decide for itself.

> Most police dogs killed in the line of duty are off-line at the time of their deaths. Many of them are out of sight of their handlers. It is argued the dogs saved the officer's lives. However, the question arises: would the suspect have confronted the dog if the handler had been with him when the confrontation took place?

Very few police dogs are killed when working on-line. Several dogs have died at the hands of suspects when they were off-line, out of sight and way ahead of the handler. In one case the dog was shot and killed. The suspect was later apprehended and had to draw a map for investigators to show them where the dog was. In another case a citizen reported he had an injured dog in his back yard. The injured dog was a police dog which was killed minutes before by a fleeing suspect. The officer was delayed crossing a fence. The dog got too far ahead and was on his own when he confronted the suspect.

In both cases the offenders had an opportunity to engage the dog alone. There was no officer to contend with and they thought they would be able to further their escape by killing the dog. In either case the officers could not have changed the circumstances – both were impeded by terrain or obstacles which prevented them from keeping up with their partner.

In speaking with armed suspects apprehended by police dogs, I have found one thing is consistent. If the dog had been alone, he would have had a battle on his hands. I have been with my dog during such confrontations, and seen suspects try to break his neck, strike him with boards filled with nails and club him with a bat. In each case I was there to help him out because I was tracking on-line.

In comparing incidents where a K9 officer was injured or killed on a track, I tried to determine whether more on-line handlers, as opposed to handlers working off-line, were injured as a result of the close proximity of the officer to their dog . Most of the incidents I am aware of where an officer is seriously injured or killed while working the dog in a tracking profile have been off-line tracks.

Also of interest is the fact that most of the dogs killed while on duty were working off-line at the time of their deaths. These incidents are attributable to both accidental deaths and deaths as a result of felonious assaults. It can be argued, however, that having the dog working way out in front of the officer is a safety margin beneficial to the officer.

In cases where the officer was shot the dog was off-line. In every single case where an armed confrontation has taken place the dog is taken out by the suspect first, with only one exception I am aware of. In that case it is unclear as to where the dog was at the time of the shooting. He may have overshot the suspect's position, drawing the handler into the suspect's range of fire. This is a concern with off-line tracking.

Both methods have their merits and drawbacks. For city work I recommend on-line work for accuracy and safety. For agencies that work a lot of rural areas, both methods would be beneficial. In many cases off-line work would gain better results. Only you can decide what method you feel the most comfortable with. Either way, be there to cover your dog. You are less likely to have a confrontation with a suspect if he has to deal with you both at the same time than if he has the opportunity to deal with you separately.

It is imperative that any application of a dog in circumstances where the dog is working in heavy traffic, or in locations such as parkades or rooftops be done on-line. Too may dogs have been lost when they have jumped over a retaining wall of a parkade or other high structure, particularly in open buildings that are near other structures. The handler's voice has a tendency to echo off adjacent buildings. In one case the dog was recalled and ran in the direction of the echo, jumping over a parkade retaining wall, and falling to his death on the street below.

Cst. Gord McGuinness of the Vancouver City Police had an incident occur where he was searching a parkade for reported car prowlers. His dog "Prince" suddenly jumped up and over the outside wall of the parkade and fell 9 metres (30 feet). Fortunately, Cst. McGuinness was working his dog on-line at the time. He was able to brace himself and secure the line, breaking his dog's fall. The harness broke from the impact of the fall, with the dog dropping another 5 metres (15 feet) to the pavement, however the harness had broken the fall sufficiently before it snapped and the dog was not injured.

Quick Reference

On-line

- Close in indications by your dog means you are within shooting range of your suspect.
- If shooting starts and you are in the open, release the dog and go for cover. He will likely be the first target of your suspect and will buy you valuable time.

Off-line

- Stay within sight of your dog. Command him to go down if necessary before he goes out of sight or if he starts to get too far ahead of you.
- Work cautiously in high traffic areas.

- Never work your dog off-line on a high building or parkade.
- Be aware your dog will frequently overshoot the suspect's location, depending on wind conditions and place you at risk of ambush.
- Try to be in a position to cover your dog. The suspect will be less likely to confront you or the dog if you are there together.

> In all cases, remove your choke collar from the dog. Whether off-line or on-line, suspects frequently have been able to grab the choke collar and twist it, momentarily gaining an advantage over the dog.

Gunfire on the Track

Should you suddenly be confronted by gunfire, if you do nothing else... move! Assess your opponent's position as you move. In most cases you will likely go to your left. Most suspects will go to ground on the right side of the track and this action alone will often put some distance between you and the offender.

When using a flashlight, shut it off immediately. Rechargeable flashlights leave a momentary tracer of light when they dim down. This can expose your direction of travel to a suspect. Point the head of the light downwards as you move to prevent him from seeing the tracer left by the light. This action will prevent the offender from anticipating your direction of travel.

Cover is a priority, concealment a minimum where cover is not practical due to your location. Engage target only if you see him. Do not waste rounds. Control your fear. You will be fine if you take control of your situation. Do not worry about your dog – let him do what he does best. He will either save your life or die trying. You must look after yourself first.

Case Study

On the 14th of September 1982 an armed robbery occurred at Albertson's food store in Bothell, Washington. A suspect wearing fatigue clothing entered the store with a .357 Magnum revolver, approached the clerk and emptied the till.

Deputy Stan Boyes, a K9 handler with the county Sheriff Department, responded to the call and arrived at the scene about 15 minutes later. Deputy Boyes learned there was a lot of contamination of the scene, however he decided to try a track anyway. An off-duty member was with Boyes and went as a back up.

Within seconds the dog picked up a fresh track and began to track on the shoulder of the roadway. As they approached an overpass the dog tracked across the highway, indicating a strong air scent. This showed they were closing in on the suspect. The dog continued the track and became excited as they started down one of the off ramps.

Deputy Boyes relates the incident in his own words:

"At this point my dog began to prance in a manner that he does when he is pretty near the vicinity of a suspect. He took us off there and went into some grass, scotchbroom, scrub alder . . . stuff like that, where he encountered a six foot high cyclone fence topped with barbed wire. These are the types of fences you find along the freeway.

When we came up to the fence he began to bark and growl, indicating very strongly towards the other side of the fence. I shone my light over the top of the dog and at that point I could see an individual with clothing which matched that of the suspect reported seen at Albertson's. I had my gun out already. The guy was crouched in the woods. He could see me then. He was on the opposite side of the fence from me.

I put my gun on him and told him to freeze, not to move . . . he ignored me, turned and disappeared farther back into the bush on the other side of the fence. At that point I picked up my K9 Chaney and threw him over the top of the fence. Deputy Onderbeke then assisted me in going over the top and indicated he was going to go around to the shoulder of the highway to try and provide some containment.

I hit the ground on the other side of the fence and was into some really thick bush. You couldn't see very far in front of you at all and right away I began looking for my dog. I called him a couple of times and he came to me, after which I started him tracking in the direction I had last seen the suspect flee. The dog hadn't gone more than three to four feet when his head came up.

At that point its kind of hazy for me. I can't remember if the dog barked or what but almost simultaneously the suspect stood up from where he had been hiding in the bush and began to shoot at me. I'm not sure how many rounds he fired at me but I believe it was one of the first two rounds that hit me. I had my gun out of the holster when one of the rounds he fired hit me. I was thrown over on my back side and while I was going down and hitting the ground I emptied my gun in the direction of the suspect. I felt I was hit pretty good. I got on the portable radio and advised there were shots fired, I had been hit and then as I recall I tried to direct some of the other deputies into containment type positions.

Once, when he shot at me on the other side, I caught just a glimpse of him either coming all the way to an upright position to shoot, or coming into a crouched type position to shoot. It was just a glimpse that I caught before the flash from both our guns kind of blinded me. Once I reloaded my gun, I got the other speedloader out and laid it beside me. I couldn't move too well, got my flashlight and just waited for the other units to come and give me some assistance."

Boyes' dog disappeared for about three or four minutes after this. It is believed he continued in pursuit of the suspect, but eventually returned to relocate his handler.

Of particular note is that Deputy Boyes had the presence of mind to secure his position first. He reloaded immediately and set up his second speed loader where it would be easy to access, given his condition. Although he does not say so in his statement, it was learned that the dense bush made it difficult for assisting officers to locate him. As they tried to find him, he shone his light upwards into the tree tops. This helped indicate his position, which eased their task. Containment was continued in the area as Deputy Boyes was transported to hospital. He received treatment for gunshot wounds to the wrist and abdomen. Although he was wearing a vest at the time, the round that penetrated his abdomen had just missed the lower corner of the armor.

Later, in the early hours of the morning, Seattle K9 Officer Belshay and his K9 Tali were continuing to work the contained area. As the dog worked along a cyclone fence the dog became excited and a short time later located the suspect lying on the ground covered in brush in an attempt to conceal himself. After a brief physical confrontation with assisting officers he was taken into custody. The officers noted that one of the rounds fired by Deputy Boyes had hit the suspect. The bullet grazed the suspect's head, but caused no serious injury. The suspect had also discarded his firearm before being found by the Seattle K9 team.

Quick Reference

When your dog indicates you are closing on the suspect:
- Shut off your flashlight.
- Move to the left of the trail and find cover. Most suspects will hide on the right side of a trail and this move alone will give you some distance between you and the suspect.
- Ready your weapon as you move.
- If your dog is released, locate him visually or by listening.
- If the dog locates a suspect, call the suspect out and order him to show his hands.
- If at all possible, try to triangulate yourself and your dog to the suspect to divide his attention.

> Remember when moving to a position, be aware of the possibility of more than one suspect being in your close proximity. Most crimes encountered are done by more than one suspect.

- Order the suspect face down in a spread-eagle fashion.
- If your dog contacts the suspect, control and cuff the suspect before calling your dog off. Maintain control and work rapidly.
- Be aware of possible setups.

9

9
Officer Effectiveness on the Track

Multiple Suspect Concerns

Often we think we are only looking for one person who has fled the scene. Most crimes are committed by more than one person. Be aware of multiple setups and never let your guard down when the dog makes an arrest. You could be ambushed by a second or even third suspect while arresting the first.

Case Study

I attended a call of a suspicious vehicle found running, parked in the driveway of a farmer's property. The vehicle had American plates and I work in a jurisdiction in Canada very near the United States border. Upon attending I learned the car had been found idling in the farmer's driveway upon his return home. The right rear passenger window was smashed out and it appeared the car was hotwired.

I unsuccessfully tried to initiate a track in an attempt to locate whoever had left the vehicle. I was alone at the time as there were no other officers available for cover. Unable to start a track, I proceeded to do building searches of all the outbuildings on the property. I searched adjacent farms and was never able to locate the individuals responsible.

I believed I was looking for the driver of a vehicle which we thought to be stolen. This was soon confirmed by our dispatch who received a message from an adjacent jurisdiction. The car had run the border crossing at their point about two hours earlier, less than six km (ten miles) from my location. I knew I was looking for one suspect for sure, possibly two suspects, and I continued my search. Afterwards I learned there were in fact three suspects who were seen in the car when it crossed the border.

I had gone to a call of an abandoned auto and ended up doing a search with my dog alone, improperly covered and not mentally prepared for more than two suspects. Again, this basic call could have turned out to be a disaster. Obviously these people were intent on fleeing. They ignored officers at the border and ran the customs gate in a stolen vehicle. Until the late dispatch came in, I only knew I had an abandoned auto that was left running in a farmer's driveway. I cannot say what would have happened had I encountered the suspects and I am glad that I did not. Always expect the unexpected and take a backup with you whenever possible.

Cuffing

A typical example of the importance of cuffing both hands and not simply cuffing one wrist to a stationary object was an incident I had several years ago. I made the typical error of being sloppy and luckily I was not hurt. However, circumstances could have been much different.

I was patrolling a residential district near a high school on night shift, when I saw a small car exit the parking lot of the school. As the car left the area I noted there was no front plate mounted on the vehicle. The car was dirty and a clean license plate was wired loosely on the rear of the vehicle. Noting the obvious possibilities I negotiated a Uturn to check the vehicle. As I did so the suspect vehicle accelerated rapidly and a short chase followed, with the driver of the suspect vehicle losing control and crashing into the front of a yard.

As I exited my patrol car I saw both suspects exit the passenger door of the car and attempt to flee. I released my dog on the lead suspect, who by now had reached the top of a ravine. At the same time I tackled the driver of the vehicle. I did not want to leave my dog vulnerable and on his own for any length of time. I quickly handcuffed the driver to his car by cuffing one wrist and locking the other cuff to the door pillar of the car.

I followed in the direction I last saw the dog and could hear him fighting with the suspect in the creek at the bottom of the ravine. When I got there the suspect was in the water up to his waist with the dog holding onto his hip. After effecting the arrest on this suspect I proceeded to help him back up the ravine.

Upon arriving near the top I was met by another officer who attended the scene as backup. There were other patrol cars now on the scene as well. I thought they had taken the driver who I had handcuffed to the car into custody as he was no longer there. However, as I approached the car I saw one handcuff was still locked to the door post of the car. The links of the cuffs had been cut and the suspect was long gone. I had only been out of sight of this suspect for about three minutes.

My first mistake was made by only securing one wrist of the suspect. This allowed him a wide range of movement. I had handcuffed him to his own vehicle, instead of taking him to a more secure position, out of reach of his car. He had in fact reached back into the car, obtained a set of bolt cutters and made good his escape almost as soon as I was out of sight. Worst of all, I did not search him before I carried on. Any one of these mistakes in themselves could have had fatal results if the suspect had access to a weapon inside the vehicle.

Bush Considerations

Many officers in rural jurisdictions often find themselves doing searches or tracks in thick, heavy bush. In some jurisdictions it is easy to pursue a suspect into thick bush and quite simply lose all sense of direction. Members of the RCMP dog services section are frequently called to work such areas and for some, a compass is a standard piece of equipment. Officers who work in the Everglades, or Fisheries officers who find themselves working in bush areas, may also find themselves in similar scenarios.

If you work in an area where your job may entail extended searches in a risky bush area, take an orienteering course and become adept at using a compass. It is not infrequent that you will find yourself searching mountain sides for convicts that are trying to elude capture.

Load Up

A more common occurrence is the pursuit of a suspect into the bush after a chase, or a track that enters into a heavily wooded area. In such cases it is easy to get turned around when the bush is very thick. The dog can be used to help you out of a bush area in many of these circumstances.

The dog can be trained to "load up" from any distance. This command is used to direct the dog to return to the patrol car and enables an officer to send his dog back to the patrol car after an incident without having to return with him. When within visual distance of the car and, there being no further need for the dog, the dog is directed to "load up." The dog returns to the car and jumps into his compartment. The officer is able to continue with whatever he is doing without leaving to put the dog in the car.

This training can be extended and is useful if the officer ever gets into heavy bush and is unsure of the way he entered. It is not difficult for K9 handlers to find themselves suddenly in the position of not knowing exactly where they are. This is more common in areas where there are no visible landmarks available. The dog is the officer's best tool in such situations – when there is no other means of locating a reference point. If the dog has been trained on extending the distance for the "load up" command, the officer can command the dog to return to the vehicle. He will backtrack his way to the car by air scenting your incoming route. All the officer has to do is follow him out. This may seem like a trivial and unlikely situation, but if you ever need to use it, you will be thankful you put the time and effort into the training.

Flare

A flare carried by the officer would be beneficial in emergencies as well. If the officer needs to pinpoint his location for surrounding officers in heavy bush areas, he only needs to fire a flare up to mark his location. In some situations, such actions could be life saving. In two shooting incidents mentioned in this book, officers were wounded, without backup in a bush area. The patrol officers had a difficult time in locating them. In one instance the officer used his flashlight to indicate his position by shining it into the treetops for the officers to see. In both cases help could have been expedited had the officer had access to a flare or similar system.

Pen Flare

A device officers might consider if they are called into a bush area would be a pen flare. The flares themselves are compact and numerous cartridges can be carried in a small case in a utility pocket. The firing mechanism is similar in size and shape to a pen and can easily clip to a shirt pocket – cheap and effective insurance for officers working in bush conditions.

Protective Glasses

Another piece of equipment that is beneficial in thick bush situations is a pair of protective glasses, similar to shooting glasses. If you know you are going to be doing a search through heavy bush, a pair of protective glasses can allow you to proceed through heavy foliage without concerns about eye damage from protruding branches. If carried in your equipment bag they are readily available should you require them.

Wire Cutters

Wire cutters capable of cutting through chain link fencing are another item that you need to have available. Frequently we enter into tracks that proceed through areas that are surrounded by cyclone style fencing. Sometimes this fencing can be a dangerous hindrance to a dog team in that the team is exposed while it tries to find a way over or around the fencing. When going after an armed suspect it is much more beneficial and quicker to be able to cut a few links out of the fence and proceed with the track. When starting a track where you know there is a lot of high fencing in the area, take a pair of cutters with you so they are available should the need arise.

Foot Pursuits

Due to the nature of our work, we frequently find ourselves in foot pursuit of fleeing suspects. The urgency of the moment usually causes officers to become sloppy. When in foot pursuit of a suspect the usual course of action is for the suspect to be fleeing and the officer to be pursuing. When an offender suddenly turns to face the officer, it goes against the officer's mindset.

When an offender suddenly changes his behavior in a manner not expected by the officer, the officer's pattern of thinking is interrupted. Without preplanning, the officer can suddenly find himself as the person who is on the defensive. *Preplanned tactics* and *foot pursuit procedures* can enhance the officers chances of survival.

Dog handlers often find themselves in foot pursuits after multiple suspects. While the dog may be able to handle one suspect, you might be required to handle a second suspect simultaneously.

Your pursuit of lone suspects is usually short because of your K9 partner's ability to quickly apprehend the offender. During such pursuits however, you should maintain your tactics in the same manner you would as if you were in pursuit of the suspect on your own.

In foot pursuits try to stay to the left, in the suspect's blind spot. Most people will look over their right shoulder when being pursued. It will also take a suspect longer to target you if armed. Most people are naturally right-handed and will have a further distance to move their hand to bring a weapon into play. If you see that the suspect is carrying a weapon, try to run on the side opposite the gun hand. Draw your weapon and mentally prepare yourself to use it. Be aware of your carry method and index your finger on the trigger guard while moving to prevent accidental discharge. If carrying an automatic, it is advisable to get into the habit of decocking between moves when moving from one position to another, if the weapon is in single-action mode.

Use of Cover

Watch for and use cover as you go. Always be aware of cover no matter where you are. If you get in the habit of looking for cover during your more routine tracks, you will find that it will become second nature to you. This conditioning allows you to respond quicker should cover be required. Never blindly follow a suspect around a corner.

> Covering a corner from a wide angle provides you with better visual advantages than using the corner for cover when in a pursuit situation.

Use quick peek techniques if you are hugging a wall. As in all situations, use this technique at different heights than normal. If your dog is with you and you are working in a stealth situation, be certain that he does not break cover before you check. It is dangerous for him and can give your position away. Make sure that he is well back from the corner before going ahead to check. Avoid releasing the dog unnecessarily, however don't hold on to him where he becomes a liability. You have to judge the circumstances according to the situation.

If shooting starts get to cover first. Return fire and then move your location if you can safely do so without compromising yourself. If your dog is sent and contacts the suspect, maintain cover. Recall your dog to you from a position of cover. Follow through with proper cuffing and search procedures, preferably with a backup officer to assist.

Practice extensively on your range, using blanks, until the procedures become second nature to you and your dog. Set up situations that include gunfights with the decoy. The scenarios can be run with known situations to familiarize yourself and your dog and then can extend into unplanned moves by the decoy. This will force you to react as the situation progresses and will teach you to be steadily aware of your cover and to react instinctively to your adversary's moves. Such training also prevents confusion for your dog when the situation arises on the street. Extend your training to live-fire exercises on strategically hidden targets to improve your shoot and move skills.

10
Building Searches

Use of K9 Units

Locating suspects in buildings is one of the more common jobs a dog team is required to do. We consider it a routine part of the job and when available, a K9 unit will respond whenever a burglar alarm is activated. The use of the dog in a building is efficient and effective when appropriately applied.

K9 officers handle so many searches as a matter of routine, they become lethargic with their attitudes on officer safety. The approach to the situation as well as the application of the dog is often tactically unsound. This is not because the officer does not know how to deal with the situation. It is usually the result of a relaxed attitude.

The next time you go into a building to search for a suspect, think about this scenario: A gas station is robbed at gunpoint by a suspect who appears agitated and unpredictable. He flees the scene and is followed at a distance by a citizen who sees him enter a nearby home. The residence is contained by patrol officers. Attempts to contact the suspect inside the home by all possible means result in no response.

In circumstances such as this, the usual course of action is to deploy an Emergency Response Team to deal with the situation. In reality, when an officer goes into a building to do a building search, he is often dealing with unknown circumstances. If he knew that an agitated and armed suspect was inside, he would call for an ERT team to do the job.

What is so different between a standard building search and the robbery situation mentioned? When an officer attends the scene of a burglary where a suspect is believed to be inside, they actually have very little information. This is particularly true on an alarm call where no suspects are seen. There is no intelligence at all about who or what you are dealing with. The officer does not know how many suspects there are or if they are armed. If they do have weapons, he will not know what type, or how many. The demeanor of the suspect is unknown. But the officer can be sure that he likely has an agitated suspect or suspects who are intent on evading arrest.

When entering a building to locate offenders, officers are doing a job based on unknowns. Given known factors the ERT team might be deployed. However, exigent circumstances dictate that unless there is a series of known factors that would justify ERT response, the dog team is called in to do the job. The officer must be mentally and physically prepared to do the job, as well as be capable of deploying in a situation that would often justify ERT response.

Approach To Building Searches

Basic rules of survival for building searches are the same as for any other application, but extra precautions are taken preparing for building work. Portable radios should be turned down, or off. Keys and coins must be secured so they are silent, and verbal communication with backup is kept to a minimum. Hand signals with backup officers are preferred and can be taught during shift briefings.

When preparing to do building searches the officer finds himself at a disadvantage. Most officers approach the point of entry to the building and shout a warning to the occupants. This affords them an opportunity to surrender before the dog is released and also warns any persons who are lawfully on the premises to identify themselves.

This verbal warning sets the stage for suspects who are inside the building hiding. You have told them you are there and that you will be using a dog to search the premises. The element of surprise is lost as they know you are about to enter. In some situations it is not tactically sound to provide warnings before entering a building. A stealth approach in many cases is wise and appropriate, notwithstanding legal requirements and department Standard Operating Procedures.

Door entries into building searches are a high risk job. Ensure you treat them accordingly, regardless of the perceived offense.

When shouting a warning into a premises which you are about to search, be sure to do so from a position of cover. One of the major mistakes made by officers is to enter the doorway when giving the warning. The dog is often released to search from a position inside the doorway. This is a fatal mistake if one or more of the suspects are armed and hiding in a high position above the doorway, or positioned on either side of the point of entry.

When giving a warning, if there is no way to do it from the entry point without proper cover, use another point of entry to start the search. A loudhailer on a patrol car can also be used to issue a warning. Treat any doorway, window or other passageway into a building, or from one room to another as a potentially lethal area.

It may be tactically sound to start a search at an entirely different point of entry from the one used by the suspects. For example, in the case of a burglary, where the suspects have smashed out the glass door at the front of the building. If a property reference is available, it is better to release the dog from another entrance that is not covered in broken glass. This prevents having to lift the dog over broken glass to gain entry, which exposes the officer and the dog. It also allows the dog to secure the chosen entry point before continuing with a systematic search. To do a proper and safe entry with a dog over broken glass is not feasible.

The escort officer covers the opposite side of the doorway as the K9 team prepares to enter. If at all possible a second backup officer should be covering from behind. When starting the search, the dog is started from the exterior of the building. This permits him to enter and clear the area immediately inside the point of entry before the officers enter the building.

Procedure

Start building searches by placing the dog in a down position close to the doorway in a manner that allows him to work scent that is exiting the building at that point. Clear the areas that must be entered first before allowing the dog to proceed any further. Teach the dog to check each door that the team must pass through by sniffing under the door and along the sides of the doorway or cracks of an open door. This may seem like basic instruction, however it is one of the most common and deadly mistakes a K9 officer makes.

Training scenarios set up by most trainers are directed towards working the dog. In building-search training, the suspects are usually hidden deep in the building. This procedure is to make the dog work the various scent cones within the building, thus exercising the dog's ability to find the suspect.

Repetitive training of this nature results in the dog consistently starting the searches well past the doorway entrance. While this is good training for scent work, it fails to condition the dog to do proper door entry routines. Training that fails to work the dog on clearing the point of entry also fails to instruct the officer in safe entry techniques.

In street situations, this training results in the dog running by the suspect with the officer following at a discreet distance. This will leave the officer exposed to possible ambush from behind if a suspect is hiding close to the point of entry.

Case Study

A building search exercise was conducted during a training conference to teach officers the problems encountered by improper building entries. In this particular building search the officer was advised there was only one suspect in the building and that the suspect was armed. The officer was directed to search the building as he normally would. Both the officer and the suspect were armed with Simunition equipped handguns with marker dye rounds.

The building used was a two-storey office and lumber yard. Inside was a narrow set of stairs that went down to a lower level. At the end of the stairs was a door that was closed but unlocked. The suspect was situated to the left side of the door, in a small room that was off the base of the stairs and in a recessed area about two metres (six feet) back from the doorway. This recessed area provided an excellent vantage point for the suspect. He was in total darkness even when the lights were on, due to shelving that cast heavy shadows in the area. He would only be visible if the officers made good use of flashlight techniques. There was no attempt made to conceal the suspect any further.

In each case the initial building entry went very well, with the officer following appropriate procedures and actions before entering. After completing the upstairs search and ensuring it was secure, the officers then approached the stairs to work the downstairs area. Their approaches were done well, with obvious concerns regarding funnel of fire problems on the stairwell. Upon reaching the closed door the officer opened the door and allowed his dog to proceed.

In most cases the officer waited a few moments before proceeding. In fifteen out of seventeen applications, the dog immediately ran ahead into a garage area and started to search rather than searching the small room that the stairs opened into. After waiting a few seconds, each officer emerged, gun in hand and quickly glanced around the corner to check for suspects. Satisfied that there was no immediate danger, the officers would then advance forward to follow the dog. In every case, although there was a clear path of sight from the officer to the suspect, the officer failed to see the suspect. As the officer entered the doorway from the bottom of the stairwell, he was "shot" in the back.

In one case, the dog immediately searched the area next to the door and apprehended the suspect without any problem. In another case, the officer waited a few moments, then being aware that the area immediately inside the doorway had not been properly cleared by the dog, called the dog back to the area of the doorway and ordered him to search again. The dog immediately keyed on the suspect and made contact.

Fifteen out of seventeen officers were shot in this exercise. None of them will ever make the same mistake again. Every officer knew at the instant they were hit by the suspect's rounds that they had made a potentially fatal mistake. Each officer was critiqued at the end of each profile and it was apparent that the lesson was well learned by each officer.

In training situations, be sure to work many setups that include one or more suspects hiding close inside the point of entry. This conditions the dog to start the search as he enters the building rather than waiting until he is well inside before starting to use his olfactory capabilities. This will also help to accustom the officer to being more aware of proper doorway applications.

The Search

Most service dogs are high energy, active dogs that are often difficult to control. Most dogs will have a tendency to run into a building using their visual senses before starting to use their olfactory capabilities. In such instances there is a high degree of chance that the dog will bypass the suspect. Do not make the mistake of doing a proper approach and then step inside the doorway or opening immediately upon releasing dog. Allow him the time to settle down to the job and clear the area before entering.

As the dog is released to begin a search, remove the choke chain from the dog and do not use any form of harness or collar on the dog. If done consistently during all training and in real life applications, it will mentally prepare the dog to building searches, just as a harness keys the dog to tracking. This is also a safety factor for the dog that prevents suspects from grabbing the collar and attempting to choke him.

Once a search is started, allow the dog to search with as little verbal encouragement as possible. Remain as quiet as possible. Always take advantage of cover in areas already cleared by the dog and be aware of where the escort officers are at all times. If unsure of how many suspects are inside the building, attempt to take a minimum of two backup officers on the search. Be prepared for multiple set ups.

Beware of the phenomenon of chimney scent. Often the dog will indicate on a wall very strongly, when it is apparent that the suspect is not there. There is no doubt the dog is working a suspect's odor, however he may very likely be picking up scent which has risen off the suspect in an adjacent part of the room. As the odor rises and strikes the ceiling, it has a tendency to drift in the direction of any air circulation and drop again as it cools.

This will often cause the dog to indicate in areas directly opposite where the suspect is hiding. This is a danger which can expose you from a direction which you are unable to determine unless you can figure out how the air in the room is circulating. Backup officers need to be educated and made aware of this type of situation. This will teach them to be aware of all the surroundings and not just the area the dog is indicating. Once it is determined the area is clear the dog must be convinced to leave it and continue until he locates the source of the odor.

When the dog locates and arrests a suspect, attention must be kept on the surrounding areas as the arrest proceeds. Once the dog is called off, the handler can cover the escort officer while the suspect is secured. Quickly interview the suspect and obtain information regarding his associates, if any. If the suspect is co-operative, determine whether or not his associates are armed and with what weapons. Escort teams can then remove the suspect to a secure location.

Provide cover to the officer as he removes the suspect and stay in a position of cover until he returns before continuing the search. Proceed in this manner until satisfied that the building is clear of all suspects.

It is not advisable to allow the dog to search a building on his own. Some agencies release the dog into a building to search on its own while the officer takes up a position of cover at the point of entry. This is particularly prominent with agencies that use the reasonable force method of apprehension. The reasoning is, the dog will not bite when a suspect is located. If the person located is the proprietor or a janitor there is less concern for liability and therefore no need for the officer to risk entering the building. When the dog locates a suspect in the building by barking and holding the suspect at bay, the officers enter the building to initiate the arrest. This method is unsound and dangerous for the officer, as well as the dog.

Short-Range Dogs

Due to the bonding process which takes place between the dog and handler, most service dogs are short-range dogs. Ranging is a term common in hunting dog circles and is related to the instinctive drives in any breed and in various types of applications. Historically, a good hunting dog is one that will not be a long ranger. If the dog ranges too far from the hunter and flushes fowl from long distances, he is of no use to the hunter, as the prey is too far away to get a good shot. For this reason the hunter desires a dog that will range shorter distances and flush the birds from a closer proximity.

Due to the training and bonding processes as well as their instinctive nature, German Shepherds, along with most other breeds used for police work, are short-range dogs. When the dog is released into a building, he will search the area that is immediately available to him. In a multiple-storey dwelling, the dog will usually only search on the floor that he is initially placed into. In a warehouse setting that is quite large, he will only cover the immediate area before returning to the handler. Thus, the building is not properly worked by the dog.

If through extensive training, the dog learns to cover a large building thoroughly without his handler as backup and locates a suspect, the likelihood of the suspect fighting and harming the dog is much greater. Should the dog locate the suspect and bark to mark the location, the handler and backup officer then have to enter the building to take physical custody of the prisoner. With this method of searching, the handler has no idea what areas have or have not been cleared by the dog. If the dog has not cleared an area they must proceed through, and a second suspect is hidden in this area, then they are putting themselves in jeopardy.

Should the dog complete the search and return to the handler, there is no guarantee that the building was properly cleared. The handler has not physically entered the building at this point to watch the indications of his dog, nor can he tell how far his dog ranged into the building. When attending officers or a property owner then enter the building to reset an alarm or proceed with the investigation, they run a chance of encountering suspects who were not located by the dog team.

Hazards

Some buildings have unique hazards the handler needs to be aware of as well. Dropoffs, catwalks, pits, pest control poisons left out in warehouses and antifreeze spilled on garage floors are only a few of the hundreds of hazards that the dog may encounter. If he is alone without direct handler supervision, the application of the dog could result in injury or death from environmental hazards, even if the alarm call the team is working on is false.

When working the dog on a building search correctly, the officer enters only the areas cleared by the dog. The search progresses in a pattern that allows each area of the building, including compartments, doors and hiding locations, to be cleared before proceeding to the next area. As the dog ranges into the next search area the officer maintains cover in an area already checked and secured by the dog.

This method is as safe, if worked properly, as waiting outside the point of entry and listening for the dog. This method ensures the officer knows what areas have been properly cleared by the dog. This also permits the officer to recall him should he encounter a danger from within the building such as a sudden drop. It also allows control of the dog if he encounters a property owner or someone who has legal right to be on the property.

During a building search the dog may find where the suspects have exited the building at a location distant from the point of entry. In such cases it is not unusual for the dog to pick up the scent and proceed out of the building to follow the suspect track.

Officers who choose to remain outside the building while the dog searches will not be aware the dog has proceeded out of the building at another point. Unless containment officers see the dog breach the building in pursuit of the suspect, the officer has no immediate information the dog has left the building. In these circumstances the dog can find himself fighting a suspect on his own, with no backup from the handler, and so is subsequently at risk.

Directing a dog in a building search should be kept to a minimum. There will be situations where the officer needs to direct the dog without leaving a position of cover. Proper direction to a specific location is often hard to do without extensive hand or voice commands. Hand signals cannot be implemented effectively in darkness. Even in daylight conditions the officer must verbally signal the dog in some way to get the dog's attention before giving a hand signal.

The flashlight can be a valuable tool in this regard. The dog is trained to cue to a search command in the direction the officer shines his light. This routine is used if the dog has missed a specific area and needs to be directed without the officer leaving cover to do so. This offers the advantage of directing the dog silently, but gives away the officer's location to the suspect. The officer should move to a new position of cover immediately if it is safe to do so.

Tips on Building Searches

- Dog leads, officer follows. Depend on the dog. Be aware of the surroundings, but always watch the dog. Trust him. Do not search one room while the dog is off in another.
- Watch the dog without getting tunnel vision. Be aware of what is above and behind.
- Stay with the dog. Search off-line and use cover while searching. Do not release the dog into a building to search on his own.
- Enter buildings from a safe point. Do not call warnings by standing in the doorway. Maintain cover at all times. Most officers have a tendency to leave their position of cover too soon, exposing themselves to unnecessary danger.
- Train the dog to check entry points first. Check all avenues of escape before proceeding to the next search area.
- Use the house lights where possible. The suspect and officer are then at the same level.
- Do not spotlight your dog with a flashlight. If you find that you must use a flashlight in a building, particularly in a large warehouse, use indirect lighting. This diffuses the light in the angle opposite from where you are. This diffused light will make it harder for suspects to pinpoint the source of the light if they do not have a direct visual on you. At the same time this method provides a large area of coverage. Use your light sparingly, in short bursts if at all possible. Remember, your night vision will be affected with each use of your flashlight.
- Don't give away your position. Work silently. Only prompt the dog verbally when absolutely necessary.
- Work exterior walls first . . . suspects have a tendency to go to outside walls in search of fast exit routes. An exception to the exterior rule is in gun shops and pharmacies. Check first the areas suspects are most likely to target. By checking these areas first, it may give you clues as to how many suspects are involved and if they have armed themselves. If you can check behind locked doors do so. If you cannot check certain rooms due to a lack of a reference or key holder, be sure you make a note of this info in your logs. It will cover you if it is later learned a suspect was behind a locked door.
- Be aware of locked areas as potential threats. An effective tool used by officers searching a building with a cement, or other hard surface floor, is to leave a coin on top of the door knob if the room is passed by. If a suspect

emerges from the room after the officer has passed by, the coin drops to the floor when the handle is turned, alerting the officer to danger. A simple but effective gimmick.

- Be conscious of the chimney effect. The suspect may be in an area opposite from where the dog is indicating. There is no way to tell which direction the scent is originating from.

- Be aware of rat poison traps and other chemicals or insecticides that may be used by the property owners. If possible, particularly in large warehouses used to store chemicals, it would be prudent to get information on the types of substances stored by interviewing the property reference. Obviously this information is not always available, but if the building is secure and there is no need for urgency, the information gleaned from the PR (property reference) may lessen risks to the dog.

- The Property Reference can provide information about the location of light switches, fans and air conditioning within the building, as well as potential risk areas. Keys to areas that offenders can lock themselves into can also be obtained to assist in clearing suspect areas.

- Locked doors or inaccessible areas are not cleared areas. These rooms could have been open when the suspects entered the building, and the suspect could have entered the room, locking the door behind him. When passing these rooms there is the potential for the suspect to come back at the officer. Those areas are potential threats to be treated accordingly should a suspect suddenly emerge from that area.

- Keep the dog's nails trim. This allows him to work a building quietly. He will also have less of a tendency to try and grip the floor with his nails when moving quickly. His attempts to extend his nails on slippery surfaces only cause him to slip more than if he is on his pads only.

11
Flashlight Techniques

Types of Flashlights

Flashlight technique is one of the least instructed areas of officer safety, yet the flashlight is probably an officer's most used piece of equipment. Dog handlers work in darkness more frequently than other officers yet very few handlers are adept with good flashlight techniques.

> Proper choice of flashlights combined with good tactics can provide a powerful tool that is vital to survival. Improper application however can be fatal.

Standard vs. Adjustable Flashlights

An officer's flashlight must be one he feels comfortable with. The K9 car should be equipped with *two* high-powered rechargeable flashlights. Due to the amount of time spent out of the vehicle on tracks, in darkness, the battery pack on a rechargeable light can be drained in a little over an hour.

At least one light is manufactured with a head that permits the officer to adjust the type of beam on the light according to his needs. This allows the officer to diffuse the light when necessary. Some officers prefer a flashlight that does not have an adjustable beam. Most officers prefer to have the light adjusted to its brightest capability and when using an adjustable beamlight the beam often has to be readjusted. With a standard head flashlight, the officer can simply grab it and go, knowing that it is perfectly focused. Another problem with some adjustable lights is a dark spot which appears directly at the centre of the beam when the flashlight is focused to its brightest position.

A disadvantage to having a standard head flashlight is that the officer cannot take advantage of diffusing the light when preferred. The light used is always a matter of personal choice. As in choosing a weapon, the officer should use what he feels most comfortable with.

A small rechargeable flashlight similar to those used for shotgun or handgun mounts for SWAT applications is ideal for dog handlers. Lights such as the Sure-Fire are compact and lightweight and still emit in excess of 20 000 candlepower in a focused beam. The Sure-Fire or its like can be carried easily on your gunbelt and is always available in an emergency. There are occasions when you will bail out of the car in hot pursuit of a suspect and neglect to grab your regular light. A Sure-Fire or other tactical high intensity light is your best backup light source. Should you drop your light during a foot chase, or have expended your regular light on an extended track, you have a light that is capable of outputting almost the same capacity of light as your regular rechargeable flashlight.

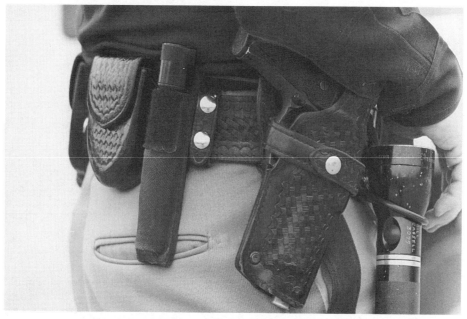

A small highpower rechargeable flashlight such as the Sure-Fire [right] is your best choice for a backup light.

Flashlight Applications

The application of the flashlight can involve various aspects in policing. It can be used as an impact weapon and a means of signaling other members. Of course its most common use in police applications is to enhance visibility. It is also used to conceal the officer's exact whereabouts by diminishing the night visibility of the person we are dealing with. This concealment should never be mistaken as a form of cover. There is a distinct difference between concealment and cover. Cover is considered any barrier that hides an officer's location and provides adequate protection from the threat he is up against. Concealment on the other hand, provides only a method of hiding your location. It does not offer any means of direct physical protection from the threat.

Criminals use darkness as a major form of concealment for their unlawful activities. They have learned that most people do not investigate things that do not appear to be out of place. Therefore, they can often work in obvious locations with a little darkness to hide their actions and never be seen by passers-by. This darkness is not a form of cover, however. It is a mask that is easily penetrated by a light source, exposing the suspect's activities. Just as this form of concealment can be penetrated by a light source, so can most any other form of concealment be penetrated by a bullet, if it is not a proper form of cover. Just because you cannot be readily seen does not mean you are out of harm's way. By the same token, just because you have no cover and only darkness or a small bush for concealment, don't suddenly decide you are fully susceptible to danger either. Both concealment and cover have their place in officer survival applications.

Whenever exiting a patrol car on a call consider the possibility that you might require your light, even under bright day light conditions. When working an urban track where the suspect(s) you are tracking have the opportunity to enter an abandoned building, subway tunnel, or other dark area, you will not be able to return to your vehicle to pick up your light. Lights are for darkness however it might occur, not just for night work.

Flashlight position during a suspect search. The suspect's concentration is on the dog, directly next to the strong light source. This keeps him distracted and inhibits his night vision.

Reflected Light

During a warehouse search an officer can take advantage of reflected light by shining his light on the ceiling, or an end wall. This action causes the light to reflect and disperse over a wide area, allowing the officer to flood the area with indirect lighting.

A frequent application of reflected light is in building searches that have bathrooms with individual toilet stalls. From the doorway, the officer can shine his light at the ceiling. The reflected light will produce shadows on the floor of the stalls if any offenders are standing on a toilet. The officer has no need to individually open each stall and reveal himself. The same technique can be used in open rooms and other search areas with the assistance of a backup officer. For example, one officer can reflect the light off a wall at the end of an aisle. A well positioned backup officer at the opposite end of the aisle will see the silhouette of anyone standing in the aisle. He is exposed from a reflected light source off the ceiling or a wall, as opposed to a direct light source. Use of reflected light in this manner makes it difficult for the suspect to pinpoint the exact location of the light source.

The use of a reflected light source can be a disadvantage. Its reflection can give away the officer's location if he is in a position that exposes him to reflected light.

Direct Lighting

Another application of lighting is that of direct light. Firstly, it offers the most effective form of lighting for visual accuracy, and thus, the best lighting conditions for the officer to see the target area in detail. Secondly, direct lighting can temporarily provide a form of concealment that can give precious seconds in which to take decisive action.

> The use of light for concealment is only effective if used in a position so as not to expose the officer.

In urgent situations he must move to a position of cover as soon as possible.

Direct lighting offers the immediate advantages of a positive light source and limited concealment, by hiding an officer's position. It also temporarily disorients the person being approached; however, it also lets the suspect know from exactly where the officer is approaching.

The suspect knows that the officer is within arm's reach of the light no matter how it is positioned from the body. Once he has recovered from the initial impact of the light's intensity, he will be likely to engage the officer if so inclined. For this reason it must be stressed that the use of the light as concealment, while effective, is a *stop gap* only.

Tactical use of direct lighting can be applied during door entries or in situations where you need to distract the offender. Rapidly flashing the beam on and off can momentarily disorient the suspect. This is a good tactical application if you must move from one position of cover to another in the dark and you need to find your way.

Shooting Techniques

Shooting techniques must be practiced in darkness with a light. A range instructor can help you adopt a style of shooting while using a flashlight, according to the weapon style you are using. A modified Weaver stance with the flashlight in the weak hand for support is effective, allows for maximum light control and supports the weapon hand. Practice extensively on the range during night shooting exercises until you are comfortable.

Use of Flashlights

In all cases, learn to use your light sparingly. Do not leave it on steady while tracking. Doing so permits the offender to track your progress and to pinpoint you as a target. Learn to work in dark conditions effectively. The same advice applies to building searches.

- Use the light sparingly.
- Use the switch on the light in a manner that it does not have to be turned fully on to operate. Short bursts of light from soft pressure on the switch can give you a good idea as to your orientation. Use it only as long as necessary.
- Night vision will be momentarily affected with any use of a light, so be aware of this before you leave any position of cover.

When suddenly engaged, if your light is in the full-on position and you drop it, you have no control over where the light shines. Should you trip and stumble, dropping your light in a building search or a track, the same scenario could occur, leaving you lighted up very nicely for your opponent. Use the light in a manner where it is operational only as long as you are putting pressure on the switch. This will prevent accidents that may expose you.

Backup

When working with a backup officer, make sure that he does not back light you and that he understands what you will be doing. Backup officers have a tendency to leave their lights on and silhouette the K9 handler from behind. It is natural for people to want to see where they are going. If your officers have not had the same experience as you in working extensively in the dark, you will find them overusing their lights. Awareness of this problem can be addressed during shift briefings. A method that is effective in getting patrol officers to learn your needs is to do training tracks at night in their area and have them work tracks with you. Make observations regarding their flashlight use and point out any obvious changes that need to be made. It will be beneficial to you both in future situations.

Being backlit by your backup officer is an invitation to disaster.

Two common mistakes officers make while working their dogs are both related to spotlighting the dog. There are times when you will have to locate your dog using your flashlight, however make the exposure to your dog brief. Officers have a tendency to keep the light on their dog throughout an entire track. This is dangerous for you and the dog.

Secondly, be aware that when you shine your light directly at your dog, if he is facing you at the time, any night vision he may have has been effectively destroyed. Try not to use direct lighting. Unlike humans, the dog does not think about how looking at a bright light source will destroy his night vision. As the light source is the brightest object to him, he will naturally look directly at the light. His night vision is just as vital to your teamwork as is yours. Keep this in mind if it is necessary to light up your partner.

Next time you are out in the field, working or training, make a mental note of your present methods. Keep track of how many times you light up your dog during a shift. It won't be long before you will realize how obvious the problem is.

Refrain from exposing your position and spotlighting your dog by overuse of your flashlight.

Quick Reference

- Use a high-powered rechargeable flashlight.
- Understand how to use reflected light.
- Do not expose yourself with peripheral light.
- Direct light can be an excellent temporary source of concealment.
- Use your light sparingly, not in full-on position.
- Do not allow yourself to be backlighted by your backup.
- Do not spotlight your dog.

12

12
Vehicle Stops

Traffic Stops

Routine car stops can become dangerous without warning, and this is when the service dog is a valuable asset. There are various methods of handler protection concerning traffic stops that can be implemented into a training program, depending on an agency's budget.

The most common method of using a dog during a car stop is having access to the dog through the open driver's window of the patrol car. The screen between the dog's compartment and the front seat is left open for access. Should the dog be needed he can exit the patrol car to aid the handler.

Parking

When parking a patrol car during a traffic stop, the handler must keep in mind the dangers to the dog should he be required to exit the car and engage a suspect. By angling the car to the right upon parking, you afford the dog protection from traffic should he be required. This also affords the officer protection from oncoming traffic, as the rear of the car is well out into the lane of traffic. However, this method fails to provide the handler with adequate cover during the initial stop, should a gunfight suddenly erupt. Risks must be assessed accordingly and the method used will depend on what the officer feels is most warranted under the circumstances.

K9 Training

The dog must be trained in how to engage a suspect who suddenly turns violent during the course of a routine traffic stop.

I have had my dog exit on the attack on two occasions where the individual I was arresting put up a struggle. I was able to handle the situation without the dog. These were both situations where it appeared to the dog that I needed help with the aggressor. In both cases I saw the dog as he came to assist and I was able to call him off and command him to reload into the car. There was a potential for liability in each case.

In another situation I was involved in a violent struggle with an impaired driver who was much larger than me. My radio failed and backup officers were unable to locate me. At one point the suspect had a hold on my sidearm and was trying to remove it from the holster. During the struggle we fell to the ground, out of sight of the dog. Although on most occasions he would have exited the car and come to my aid, he failed to do so this time. He had exited the car prematurely in a previous incident I described earlier. After being returned to the car on that occasion, it made him hesitant to exit during this incident.

During the confrontation, my dog was barking, the suspect was screaming, and in all the commotion the dog could not hear me calling for him. It was apparent that he was unsure as to what to do, agitated as he was. After fighting for about three minutes, I broke away from the suspect, ran back to the patrol car with the suspect in pursuit and physically opened the rear door to the dog's compartment. The incident quickly turned around at that point.

In 1990 another incident in Broward County, Florida, resulted in the death of a K9 Officer when he left his dog in the back of his patrol car. There was no access left open by the officer and the dog was unable to exit to help the handler.

A preferred method of protection is the use of a system which gives you remote access to your dog. K9 Lifesaver by Radiotronics Inc. gives distinct advantages over leaving the window down for the dog. This unit allows maximum control of the dog by the handler.

K9 Lifesaver

The K9 Lifesaver is a device that can greatly reduce potential liability to law enforcement agencies as well as protect the officer. The Lifesaver is a gas spring mechanism that pushes the door open and holds it open when activated from a remote transmitter worn by the dog handler. It gives the officer the choice as to when the dog is needed instead of the dog trying to discern when he is required. This prevents confusion for the dog when he is corrected for leaving the car prematurely and so consequently fails to exit the patrol car when he is needed.

The system allows the officer to leave the vehicle with the windows up, keeping the air conditioning running and the temperature in the car consistent in hot summer months. There is no concern about liability with a premature exit of the dog from the car and there is no confusion for the dog as to when he is needed.

Although Lifesaver can be installed on any door in the patrol car, it is best equipped on the passenger side dog compartment. This allows the handler to park the patrol car in a manner that allows maximum protection from the offender's vehicle with the nose of the car into the lane of traffic and the engine block between the patrol car and the suspect's vehicle. When the unit is activated and the door opens there will be no danger of the door swinging open into oncoming traffic. This permits a safer exit for the dog as well.

When equipped with the door opening device Lifesaver, the officer must be aware of where he parks his patrol car. Should the device be triggered in an emergency, the patrol car needs to be clear of other parked cars or any other objects that might hinder its operation if the car is too close.

Window Drop

Another option to the Lifesaver device is a remote window drop. This device can be installed to allow the dog to exit the patrol car via any chosen window that he is conditioned to respond through. Benefits of the window drop are that the officer never

K9 Lifesaver by Radiotronics permits the officer to remotely release his dog from the patrol car in an emergency.

has to be concerned about the door opening into traffic. There is no concern about finding himself inadvertently stopped too close to a barricade, car or other object that would prevent the door system to operate.

The best system for installation is the remote door opening system. There is less likelihood of the dog being injured by an improper exit from the vehicle, which sometimes occurs when a dog exits the patrol car window at a steep angle.

The Radiotronics Lifesaver has built in safety features that provide benefits and safety features which are a must for this type of system. The door release is disabled while the patrol car is in motion. This prevents accidental activation of the unit while driving, which could open the door and result in the injury or death of the dog. The transmitter itself is small, allowing the officer to easily carry it on his equipment belt or in a shirt pocket. It has an effective range of 120 metres (four hundred feet) from the patrol car. The opener is operated with a gas spring that pushes the door open and secures the door open after the dog is released. This prevents the door from swinging open and then bouncing shut on the dog as he is exiting the car. This provides for a safer and complete opening of the door. Each device is equipped with an optional system that allows installation on cars with electric door locks in a manner which first unlocks and then unlatches the door. There is never a concern about inadvertently leaving the doors locked and the dog not being able to respond in an emergency.

Training for the dog must be provided to teach him to exit the vehicle on the right and come around the front of the patrol car when needed. Due to the lack of reasoning power in the dog, his natural inclination will be to concentrate directly on the source of the problem. It will sometimes take a bit of conditioning to teach the dog to respond to a threat by turning away from it to exit the car.

Training with the Lifesaver should teach the dog to respond immediately when the door opens. He exits the patrol car on the right and proceeds to the front of the vehicle on the right side of the patrol car. The dog will master the routines in most cases, in a very short time. Training can then progress to increase the distance he must respond as well as the locations around the vehicle where confrontations could occur. This will further condition the dog to respond, for assistance via the shortest route possible once he has exited the patrol car.

High Risk Vehicle Stops

Felony vehicle stops are becoming commonplace and proper use and control of the dog in such stops is required for the safety of all involved. If the dog is not trained to perform in a manner that is efficient when needed and quiet when not required, the dog can in fact become a liability during a high risk stop. When trained and applied properly, however, the dog can be a valuable asset.

Initiating a Car Stop

When the dog unit initiates a car stop, the officer must approach the situation in the same manner as any patrol officer would without a dog. This includes:
- proper vehicle placement
- use of appropriate cover
- verbal commands
- control of the suspect vehicle

Control of the K9

The dog is an added concern. If he is out of control, barking in the rear compartment while the officer initiates the stop, he can become a liability. During a car stop, the dog must be quiet in order for the handler to properly control the situation. It allows the officer to hear any verbal communication coming from the suspect vehicle, as well as communication from fellow officers on the radio. A noisy dog in these circumstances causes confusion and is a distraction, which the officer does not need.

Proceed the same as any felony stop. The commands to the suspects must be concise and clear. Orders must be chosen carefully and care must be taken to be sure the suspects comprehend them.

Backing Up a Car Stop

Preferably, a dog unit attending a felony car stop as a backup unit should be positioned as the third car on the scene. This allows the handler to concentrate more on the dog and be better prepared to apply him if an occupant bolts and runs from the suspect vehicle. The dog should be in a *down stay* position in the rear compartment of the patrol car to keep him out of immediate targeting by any suspects should the officer remain in his vehicle during the stop. If the officer has a well controlled dog in this type of a situation, he will be at a distinct advantage.

Should a suspect bolt from the vehicle while the K9 unit is the only vehicle on the scene, the decision to deploy the dog must depend on the situation. If the dog captures the suspect close to the felony vehicle, the officer can still concentrate on the vehicle occupants and maintain verbal control of the dog. If the dog is deployed over a longer distance the officer must concentrate on the vehicle occupants and let the dog do his job. The officer cannot afford to take the risk of having his concentration taken off the suspects still within the vehicle, or gamble that the vehicle's driver, which his dog is pursuing, is in fact the only occupant of the car simply because he was the only one visible. In such cases it is neccesary for the officer to wait for backup attendance before backing up his dog. Ideally, the best situation is to have the dog deploy as quickly as possible.

If the K9 unit is not one of the primary units in a felony stop, it can be set up as the third car on the scene, offset to the rear and slightly to the right of the primary vehicle, or fanned out to the left of the primary vehicle. The K9 officer can exit his patrol car, remove the dog and move quickly to a position of cover behind his patrol car.

The dog is placed in a down position behind the rear of the car. This affords the team good cover, and the K9 officer can observe the driver's side of the suspect vehicle or have clear coverage of the passenger side, depending on vehicle placement.

Once the car is cleared of suspects the dog can be deployed to search the car for other suspects who might be hidden. It is not recommended as a method of routinely clearing cars that are likely to have armed suspects lying in the rear seat. Once all other avenues of checking the vehicle for further suspects have been attempted, a well-directed dog will indicate if someone is still concealed in the vehicle. If necessary, he will also engage the individual, allowing officers to move in. The dog can also be used to indicate if there is someone concealed in the trunk to better prepare you for clearing that area as well.

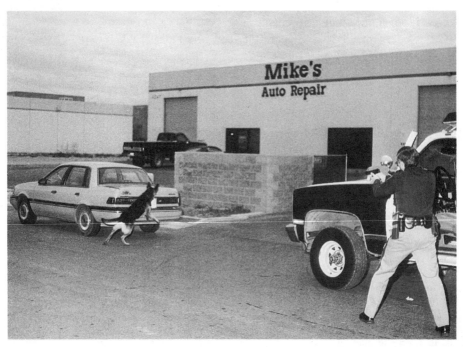

A properly trained dog can be deployed to check a felony vehicle to see if there are any suspects still inside. In this case the dog is indicating very clearly a suspect concealed in the trunk.

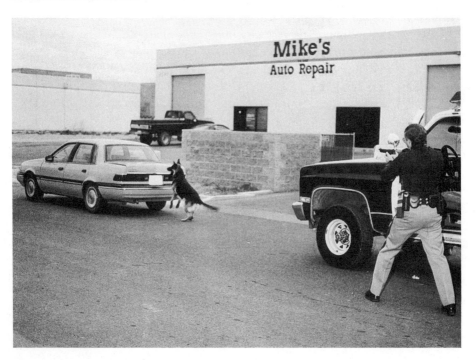

Car Clearing and Chemical Agents

Although felony car stops are handled by regular patrol officers, the use of a dog familiarized with car clearing and chemical agents can be a valuable asset when dealing with dangerous situations. Most patrol teams usually handle felony car stops without the use of a dog team quite effectively. However, progressive dog handlers are now teaching their dogs to assist in clearing vehicles of suspects who are concealed in areas of the car not easily visible to the officers. If a suspect is hidden in the trunk or rear seat of a vehicle, the dog is used to inform the officers of the hidden person.

The usual method of clearing the rear seat of a vehicle requires that an officer get into a position that enables him to see into the vehicle. Often this cannot be done without coming into close proximity to the suspect car, therefore putting the officer in jeopardy. Should a suspect refuse to leave his position of cover from the floor of the rear seat compartment, a dog can be effectively applied to extricate the suspect. The dog should never be sent to apprehend an armed suspect from a vehicle without proper deployment of backup officers and the application of chemical agents. To do so will likely result in the unnecessary death of the dog.

K9 deployed to extricate a suspect unwilling to step out of his vehicle.

When it is determined that a suspect is refusing to exit the vehicle and a decision is made to apply a dog for the extrication, a chemical munitions agents expert should fire enough CN or CS agent into the car to disable the suspect. Wait an appropriate time for the suspect to surrender. If the suspect fails to comply with requests to surrender, another volley of gas is fired and the dog is immediately applied to extricate the offender. Chemical agents are seldom used in such situations, yet are a valuable asset in reducing risks. There is no reason why an armed suspect in a vehicle should be treated any differently than an armed and barricaded suspect in a building. Chemical agents are frequently used in buildings, yet they are rarely if ever applied to armed suspects in felony vehicle stops, often because a gas technician is unavailable. But chemical agent application should be considered if adequate resources are available.

Case Study

Recently, I was called to assist in an adjacent city, in a situation which resulted in the takedown of two vehicles that were gang-related. The occupants were believed to be armed. The suspects in one vehicle were stopped by the team I was with, while the second car was located and stopped a few blocks away. Afterwards we learned that a suspect in the vehicle stopped by the second team had remained hidden on the rear floor of the vehicle until physically approached and removed by the officers. This would have been a perfect application for chemical agents backed by use of a dog.

In vehicle pursuits and bailouts it is imperative that the car be checked and secured before running by it in pursuit of any suspects. The dog can be sent after the fleeing driver or other running suspect.

> Never run by the suspect vehicle in pursuit of the dog. Never run by or approach an unsecured vehicle.

This seems like common sense, but in the heat of the moment we have a tendency to forget basic survival skills.

A common occurrence during car stops. The driver and lone occupant of the vehicle flees a car, later determined to be stolen. The dog is sent and the officer pursues.

The potential dangers of such a move. Officers have lost their lives when an unseen assailant suddenly emerges and fires on the officer. Never run by an unsecured suspect vehicle.

In Edmonton, Alberta, a robbery occurred where the suspects fled the scene in a car. In the ensuing search for the vehicle, a member of the Emergency Response Team on patrol saw the suspect vehicle turn up an alley, and pulled behind the car to follow. As the car proceeded up the alley, it was obstructed by heavy trucks being loaded. Having no place to go, the suspect driver stopped his car and stepped out.

The officer immediately drew his weapon and covered the suspect, ordering him to put his hands up. The suspect complied as requested. The officer then left his position of cover in his car and started to approach the suspect. As he neared the suspect, a second unseen accomplice sat up in the back seat of the car and killed the officer with a single shotgun blast.

Although this is not a dog application scenario, it is an example of how a well-trained officer easily forgets basics. Never leave a position of cover until appropriate backup has arrived and the suspect vehicle is properly cleared. The dog will handle himself. Because of liability concerns, officers are often too quick to pursue their dog in order to recall him as soon as the suspect gives up. Officers are trained to call the dog off the suspect once the apprehension is made in order to protect the dog and prevent unnecessary injury to the suspect. In situations where the handler has to expose himself to an unchecked vehicle, the priorities must change in order for the officer to protect himself. The officer's first priority must be for himself. Worry about the dog and the suspect later.

If in an open position where there is no protected position from which to observe or clear the interior of the vehicle, the officer can make use of the patrol car as "rolling cover." This is done by having an officer lie on the front seat and slowly drive the patrol car up beside the suspect vehicle. A second officer walks alongside the car on the driver's side (the side furthest away from the suspect vehicle), in a crouched position at the front wheel area, and covers the suspect vehicle with a shotgun. The second officer can be backed up by a third officer maintaining cover behind the driver's pillar. The patrol car rolls forward into a position beside the suspect car, where the officers can clear it, and the two officers walk slowly beside the police unit, using it for cover as it moves forward. Once the suspect car is cleared, the handler can then proceed to back up his dog.

Quick Reference

- A quiet dog is vital during felony vehicle stops.
- Maintain cover.
- Set up as the secondary, or even third unit on the scene whereever possible, so you can concentrate on using your dog.
- Use the dog to assist in clearing the vehicle after all visible suspects have been extricated.
- Never run by an uncleared felony vehicle.

13

13
Emergency Response Team Support

Training For ERT

Training of an ERT dog must include every member of the team. Each member must become familiar with the dog and be able to take over in case of an emergency. As the dog handler must be fully trained in ERT tactics, every member of the team should be given a basic handler's course. This will enable him to work the dog and control him if the handler is neutralized during an application.

Vancouver City Police Emergency Response Team in British Columbia, Canada, working in co-ordination with the K9 Unit.

Command Language

I have heard many arguments about the use of German commands as opposed to English commands for the training of patrol dogs as well as ERT dogs. Some say when the suspect hears the dog commanded in English it warns the suspects the dog is there. Some state that a suspect could confuse the dog by trying to command him if the dog uses English commands – when the dog is trained initially, exercises should be performed that require the dog to respond to commands given only by the handler.

For example, a group of dogs going through training together are placed side by side in a group. Each dog has been successful in learning to stay in a long down position over an extended period of time. Each handler takes turns trying to entice the other dogs to break their position by calling each one, coaxing him or rolling a ball in front of him. Any break by the dog is met with a correction from a handler. Conversely, any success by the dog is rewarded. This training can be progressed further if desired by having your training decoys try to give commands to the dog while the dog is attacking.

The discipline the dog develops prevents another person from interfering by giving contradicting commands. In my personal experience, I have never yet had a situation where my dog even hesitated when confronted by a suspect screaming orders at him.

I recommend the use of the language in which the handler is most familiar to train the dog. In most cases around North America, that is English, Spanish, or French. A properly trained animal will not have to receive loud commands and in fact should be signal-trained for work under strict conditions. The reason for using native language is that a person's natural tendency in an emergency is to revert to his own language. If you train your partner in German commands and suddenly need to call him back under fire, it is likely that under pressure you will call out to him in English. For this reason I strongly recommend using commands natural to you.

Do not be concerned if you have a dog that has been started in German, Dutch or French. If your natural language is different, take the time to convert the dog. It is easy for the dog to learn. By using consistency and allowing for time to familiarize the dog with the new language, a sharp dog is easily converted in four to six weeks.

Stealth Approaches

Stealth approaches are a method commonly used in Canada to isolate suspects within a specific room in a building. The dog is worked on-line, in a harness. The dog team is then used to search the building to locate the room in which the suspect is hiding. Once the dog has determined the room, he is pulled out of the situation and used only as a rear guard, or removed entirely. The response team, now knowing exactly where the suspect is located, proceeds to follow through with actions deemed neccesary according to the situation. During this exercise the dog works quietly, without barking, growling, or making any form of verbal communication. The dog's body language is read by the handler to allow the team to remain somewhat undetected.

Corporal Al Girard, an ERT team dog handler, deployed with members of the Royal Canadian Mounted Police ERT team in response to a barricaded gunman call. After exhausting all attempts to contact the suspect, the ERT team made an entry into the residence, using the dog on a stealth approach. The handler advised the officers which room the suspect was in and in fact, from reading the body language of the dog, was able to advise them that the suspect was dead. The ERT team moved into position, did an entry on the room and found the suspect deceased from a self-inflicted gunshot wound.

Visual vs. Olfactory Sense

One of the key factors in the use of ERT-trained dogs is the use of the dog's visual senses as opposed to his olfactory capabilities. The dog's natural inclinations are to use his nose more than his eyes to search for suspects. In ERT situations, however, you are using a combination of both.

When training for ERT, your dog has to be able to switch between visual and olfactory capabilities quickly. Initially, if using the dog in dynamic entry situations, the dog is trained to visually look for a suspect. Again, this is contradictory to normal street situations, which usually require the dog to use his olfactory capabilities when entering a building. For this reason training with ERT members in building entries is important in familiarizing the dog with situations that will condition him to work visually or in stealth mode when required. For this reason, it is becoming more popular to use dogs assigned for ERT response only for these assignments, instead of dogs also used on the street for patrol purposes.

ERT Training

Preparation for ERT takes months of training the team as a whole, as well as training the dog and handler individually. *Conditioning* and *consistency* are the keys. Initial training can involve using a decoy in a full bite suit standing outside the doorway of a building for the dog to take down. After the takedown the decoy steps inside the doorway and the dog is sent on the attack, learning that there is always something just inside the door under certain circumstances. Continue to extend the training so the suspect is standing in different positions within the room and at different depths from the entrance. Extend the capabilities by changing your situation to different buildings and room types. Deploy the dog from outside the building as well as inside. This room-clearing technique must be exact if you are to employ the dog in an effective manner.

Once you have mastered room clearing visually, you must continue to work your dog in situations where he has to revert to using his olfactory capabilities. Once ERT has neutralized a suspect, the building is not considered secure until the rest of the residence is cleared. The dog is used to determine the location of any other suspects. This requires the dog to use his olfactory capabilities to search for hidden persons. Again, the dog must be able to switch from one mode to the other almost instantly. The natural inclination of the dog is to use his nose if he loses sight of the suspect. Keep this in mind when setting up your target. The following example might aid in demonstrating.

Case Study

I responded to a call reporting a distraught man. The man, upset over the breakup of his family, had a loaded rifle. At the time of the call, the man's four-year-old boy was in his custody and there was concern for the boy's safety. The little boy at one point walked out and rode his bike towards officers who were in the area and was immediately apprehended.

Shortly afterwards the man came out through the sliding glass doors to call for his son. Receiving no reply, he continued out towards a roadway. There was a large eight foot hedge blocking the suspect from our view and we were in a position only 10 metres (30 feet) away. Another officer at an observation point saw the suspect leave the rifle inside the apartment; however, it would only take two strides for the man to get to the weapon. We waited until the suspect walked out from the hedge area about three metres (10 feet) from the hedge, when he was confronted by one of our ERT members. At the same time, I deployed at a position which was angled so that if the man ran around the hedge, he would still be in view of the dog.

If the suspect had bolted for the rifle and the dog lost momentary sight of him, he might not have had enough time to target the man before the rifle was brought into play. Once the man had vaulted the ground floor balcony, it is very likely the dog would have been delayed somewhat as he tried to work the situation out, momentarily using his nose as opposed to his eyes. In such situations split seconds count. In this situation the man was taken into custody without incident.

Familiarity of Team Members

Familiarization with the sudden and sometimes odd movements of ERT team members is vital to the proper use of the dog. The way members crouch and crawl could be a sign to the dog that these people are offenders.

Familiarize him with each member and their movements. This should be done while the officers are in normal clothes and also while they are equipped with nomex hoods and masks, so this becomes a natural way of working for the dog. Have each member throw a ball for the dog during break times and ensure that each member plays with the dog during every training session, so he becomes familiar with each person's demeanor and scent characteristics. Every officer should take steps to become one of the dog's best friends. This familiarity will allow the dog to work with the team without any fear of him mistaking the actions of any of the team members as offensive during an operation.

These are only a few of the basics and should only be considered an overview. Be sure the dog is trained in a diversified set of circumstances. In no way should these routines be attempted without proper study and training by authorities in the field. Also, as a dog handler, you know the limitations of both yourself and your dog. Take the advice I give any street officer and every K9 officer I ever train: Never take on a task you feel that you or your partner cannot handle.

Narcotic Raids

The dog team is best used as rear security on drug raids.

> Refrain from being the first one through the door, since there is too high a possibility of the building being booby-trapped.

Drug entries require human intervention first. To use a dog on a door entry in a drug raid situation may be an invitation to disaster.

As in ERT applications, the quiet dog catches the suspect. Work on long *down stays* when training for this type of work. Practice with the Drug team so your dog is used to the officers and their procedures. He must learn that they are part of his team and the officers must be aware of how to co-ordinate with the K9 team. Use your patrol dog to search the house for hidden suspects once all known occupants have been removed. Beware of hiding places in false ceilings, walls and floors. A separate dog should be used to do the drug searches. A dog that is excited from doing an entry and search for suspects will have a hard time settling into a methodical drug search.

Antidote Kit

Whenever called into a drug search, ensure you carry a fully equipped drug antidote kit for the dog in your personal equipment. Should the dog ingest any narcotics during a search, it is not practical to take the time to run to the patrol car to get the antidote. You will need to administer it at the scene immediately.

Poisonous Snakes

If you note caged mice in the residence, they could be an indication of poisonous reptiles used to guard the contraband. These mice are used to feed the snakes, so beware during your investigation.

14

14
Chemical Agents

Applications of Chemical Agents

The use of chemical agents is widespread in today's law enforcement. Chemical agents are extremely effective in one-on-one confrontations, crowd control and barricaded suspect situations. Often the effectiveness of dogs combined with chemical agents is overlooked by agencies, particularly in the areas of crowd control and barricaded suspects.

As the use of dogs becomes more prevalent in ERT situations, the aspect of combining effective chemical munitions with the dog is becoming an extremely effective and life saving combination. The information contained here is only an outline. No K9 unit should implement the use of dogs and ERT or chemical munitions without proper and extensive supervised training through an experienced agency.

There are various methods of disseminating gas in a given situation, including foggers, pyrotechnics, expulsion, etc. The method of disbursement will not be covered here. The officer should be aware, however, that he will be required to deploy his dog in various types of situations. Each circumstance will dictate what form of disbursement will be used. As such, during training profiles officers need to familiarize the dog with each method of dissemination used within their department.

Chemical agents come in various types, CN (Chloroacetophenone), CS (Orthochlorobenzalmalononitrile), DM (Diphenylamine Chlorarsine) and more recently Capsicum (Oleoresin Capsicum). Both CN and CS agents can be used in co-ordination with the dog team, providing the chemicals are dispersed properly, according to the situation.

Capsicum, on the other hand, is not only effective against humans, but has a profound effect on dogs. Capsicum at a 1 per cent concentration is commonly sold to knock down dogs. Most Capsicum concentrations for law enforcement use are 5 percent, a substantially stronger concentration. If a dog is to be deployed into a situation, Capsicum-based agents cannot be used.

Lacrimators

Both CN and CS agents are called lacrimators, that is, they attack the lacrimal system of the body. This is the group of organs that produce tears to keep the eyes moist and protect them from dust and other irritants. The lacrimal gland is positioned in the upper, outer corner of the eye. Its ducts excrete a constant stream of tears that wash the eye and drain through two openings located in the inner corner of the eye. These openings drain into the lacrimal canaliculus, then into the lacrimal sac and into the nasolacrimal duct, ending in the nasal cavity. When a lacrimator is discharged, the effect is profound irritation of the eyes and mucous membranes. This forces the eyes, as well as other areas of the body prone to sweating (such as the groin and armpits), to burn.

The dog, unlike a human being, has no lacrimal system. Lacrimators will not affect him in the same way. As his mucous membranes are not interfered with in the same manner as humans and he has the ability to see as well as normal, the dog can enter a building to visually locate an offender. He still has full use of his olfactory system and can search for a hidden offender. This is not to say that the dog is not affected by the chemical agents at all. Too high a concentration of the product or extended exposure can cause ill effects. However, properly applied agents in controlled circumstances will not adversely affect his abilities.

CN Agents

CN agents will not usually affect a dog in lower concentrations. He will usually perform in CN gas in the same way he would under clear circumstances. CN is toxic in high concentrations. The dog has a 16 percent higher lethal tolerance to this product than humans.

> CN is the recommended gas for K9 applications where the dog may be required to work under gas conditions for an extended period of time.

An example is the search of a building for an armed suspect, where the dog is required to use his olfactory system to determine the suspect's location.

CS Agents

CS agents will affect the dog and must be used with caution. CS gas is less toxic to humans than CN gas, but more effective. The dog can work within the CS environment, but not for as long a time as is possible with CN agents. If CS agents are used, the dog will be able to work in this environment without adverse effects if the application is not over an extended time.

Smoke

One aspect of special agents that is not often practiced with the dog is that of smoke applications. Many dogs do not like smoke and will often show avoidance when confronted with it. Experiments have shown most dogs to be unsure when entering into a thick fog of smoke, even when on lead with the handler. Spend time on familiarizing your dog with smoke.

Because smoke is not an irritant, as are the various forms of gas, officers have a tendency not to train with it. They do not realize that the visual effect of the smoke screen will often cause more problems when applying a dog than CS or CN agents. In the field when the dog is sent into smoke conditions, the dog fails to perform as he did in training situations if he has not been worked extensively in smoke disbursement. An actual deployment is a dangerous time to have the dog turn back on the handler.

For this reason, when choosing a form of disbursement, ferret rounds are recommended. Ferret rounds disseminate evenly through the intended area and do not disperse smoke. Disbursement methods combined with smoke can only be used if the dog is properly familiarized with them.

In training, include applications involving searches under cover of smoke to help lessen the dog's hesitation – he's apprehensive because the smoke appears to be a solid wall. If the handler enters the smoke with the dog, the dog will usually enter the smoke without difficulty. However if the dog is directed into a smoke-filled area without any form of support from the handler, he will often stop short of entering the smoky area. It takes extensive training in smoke applications for most dogs to perform reliably.

Gas Technicians

When developing a training program with chemical munitions, supervision from a gas technician is necessary. Gas technicians are trained in the proper methods of applying gas in a given situation and are familiar with toxicity levels. The technician can calculate how much agent to use, depending on the area to be covered, and can help to safely put together a chemical agent training program.

When the dog has been introduced to chemicals in controlled conditions, the next step is to practice under street situations. Here it is important for the dog to understand the handler's signals to prevent confusion. When a dog team begins training for door entries and high-risk work, they must train with the ERT team or backup officers they will be supported by.

The key to successful deployment is familiarization through repetitive training of the team as a whole. The dog must learn team members are working with him, and not focus on them as the aggressors. It takes hundreds of hours of training to achieve a level of reliability before the dog can be realistically applied. The dog must also become familiar to discerning commands through the handler's gas mask.

Training includes room assaults using a decoy and the entire team. This builds confidence among team members and prevents confusion in real deployment. Room entries are usually preceded by a flash bang or other method of diversion. When training, the flash bang must be implemented as it would in a real scenario. This accustoms the dog to the noise and unusual circumstances. Consistent training in this procedure will result in the dog keying to the flash bang as a *"GO"* signal. Over a period of time the dog's performance will become second nature and a valuable asset to any ERT team.

K9 Maintenance Chemical Decontamination

It is important that the dog be carefully decontaminated after any chemical application. The agents are toxic and need to be thoroughly removed from the dog's coat. This is not only for the comfort of the dog, but also for the comfort of those he contacts subsequent to the application.

To help in cleansing the dog's coat after an application, each dog car should be equipped with a five-gallon jug of water secured in the trunk. This can be used for drinking water for the dog and is also ideal for rinsing the dog after exposure to chemical agents.

When exposed to chemical agents, the dog should be rinsed with cool water. Large quantities of running water are preferred. The water carried in the patrol car will probably be insufficient to do a complete job. The dog's coat should not be rubbed while rinsing. Most of the agent will be on the exterior of his coat and rubbing his coat will only cause the agent to work its way into the dog's skin. Rinsing will take most of the irritants out of his coat and is strongly recommended prior to placing the dog back into a patrol car. A preliminary washdown can be given at the scene with the water supply from the vehicle. A more thorough cleansing from a hose with running water should follow as soon as possible.

Quick Reference

- Avoid Capsicum (oc) based products with dog teams.
- CS/CN recommended for use when combined with dog teams.
- Always use the services of a qualified gas man.
- Dog must be able to understand the handler through the gas mask.
- Hand signals recommended.
- Proper decontamination of the dog is required upon completion of deployment.

15

15
K9 Testimony

Courtroom Testimony

Courtroom testimony is where the true test of street work comes together. The training and application of the dog is scrutinized in fine detail in the courtroom. If an attorney can prove that the application of the dog was improper or if he can raise any doubt about the continuity of the tracking evidence, the officer stands a good chance of losing the case.

Officers must be concerned about the contact the dog makes with the accused and be able to justify that contact. Credibility is the key to success in the courtroom. Many good programs have been discontinued because of improper applications by K9 officers, or by the appearance of improper applications. Many officers boast about the damage done to a suspect by their dog. Others key the mike open to allow others to hear the dog getting his "justice" at the end of the track. This type of behavior leaves the department as well as the officer open to a lawsuit and undermines the officer's credibility.

Defense attorneys are starting to subpoena radio tapes of incidents for court purposes. If the officer is not acting in an efficient and professional manner, his credibility will be questioned in court. Credibility lies in the quality and results of arrests. Suspects will even comment on the dog's abilities when handled in a professional manner.

On more than one occasion I have captured offenders who were bitten by my dog and subsequently commented on his abilities. One backup officer advised me, after a track that resulted in the apprehension of a drug suspect, that the offender kept saying, "Smart dog, smart dog," as he was being escorted back to the perimeter. I have even had suspects comment on how under control the dog was when I called him off the bite.

Your level and abilities as a handler will always be probed by defense counsel. Do not give them any fuel for their fire. Work your dog and perform in a professional manner. Avoid allowing your dog unnecessary or extended bites. Be sure that your suspects obtain medical treatment immediately before taking them to jail. Your concern for their welfare once you have them in custody will go a long way in boosting your credibility in court.

Admissibility of Tracking Evidence

Once in the courtroom you are in another realm in which you need to survive. There are five points that most courts require to obtain admissibility of tracking evidence.

1. Handler is qualified by training and experience to handle the dog and interpret his actions.
2. The dog is adequately trained to track human scent.

3. Experience shows the dog has been a reliable tracker of human scent. (This is where the value of a dog log is invaluable.)
4. The dog was placed on the track where circumstances indicated the suspect had been.
5. The trail left by the suspect was not so stale and contaminated so as to interfere with the accurate ability of the dog to track.

Résumé Preparation for Court

Prepare a résumé listing your training and years of experience and books read, as well as courses and seminars attended. When you attend court have a booklet of your résumé prepared in multiple copies so you may distribute one each to the prosecutor, defense attorney and the judge if required. If you are at a jury trial, have a booklet prepared for the foreman of the jury as well. By having multiple copies of a well-prepared résumé ready, you demonstrate your expertise and efficiency to the court.

DOs and DON'Ts of Court Appearances

Do:

- In preparation for court, review any tapes that you may have of the occurrence.
- Be sure when you are putting your case together that you have enough evidence to corroborate your case.
- When giving your evidence, maintain your objectivity and professionalism. Avoid any appearance of accusation through your testimony. For example, some officers testify regarding the theory that a person under stress gives off different pheromones than when under normal conditions. This is often called "fear scent." When giving testimony in regards to this type of scent, avoid using any terminology that might construe guilt. Evidence that a suspect is giving off a fear scent is considered an opinion of the officer by most courts and in most cases is frowned upon by judges. Use the term "enhanced scent" when you testify. This is professional and shows your objectivity to the court and increases the credibility of your evidence. This is not to say that you cannot then elaborate on what causes enhanced scent and how it is produced if prompted by the prosecutor or asked by an attorney.
- You can say, however, that you did a track with your dog that resulted in the successful apprehension of the accused. You arrested the accused based on the information provided to you by attending officers or witnesses. It is up to the courts to put together the continuity of evidence that led up to your track. This again will show your objectivity and credibility.

- Have an established list of questions in a handout to give the prosecutor before court time. The questions on the list establish all the issues required to admit the five major points. Following is a such a list, a series of predicate questions which establish the groundwork for your evidence.

Don't

- Take your dog to court unless directed by a judge to do so. Any demonstrations need to be performed on neutral territory.
- Go to court with a weak case even if your dog was successful. You run the danger of losing the case and the possibility of creating bad case law. In the long run that result can hurt more than letting one case go. A dog track is often probable cause to arrest, but not enough to convict.
- Your evidence cannot be that the person your dog apprehended is responsible for the crime committed, unless you saw the crime take place and you can identify the accused.
- Allow yourself to be qualified as an expert by defense counsel without going through your qualifications. Be sure the prosecutor still goes through the process of qualifying you, particularly on a jury trial. This allows you the opportunity to impress upon the judge and jurors the level of your expertise. The result is that your evidence is given more weight.
- If pressured by defense attorneys, never get defensive about your dog. Be positive and maintain cool, professional composure. Do not trap yourself inadvertently. For example, there are alarm companies that set up clients' properties so when an alarm is triggered, the operator can listen in at the client's property. These occurrences are often taped. When you attend the call and then put your dog out to search the building, be aware that your actions may be monitored and taped. During a court case, an attorney asked the officer if he called a warning into a school he was searching before releasing his dog into the building. The officer was adamant that he had given three verbal warnings prior to releasing the dog on the search. Unknown to the officer, the defense attorney had subpoenaed the alarm company's tape of the incident. The tape was produced and played for the court. It became quite clear that no warning was given. This situation destroyed any credibility the officer may have had.

Questionnaire to Establish Expert Evidence in Tracking

1. State your full name and rank.
2. What is your occupation and who is your employer?
3. Length of present employment?
4. What is your current assignment and length of time in that assignment?
5. What other assignments have you had during your career?

6. What formal training have you had as a dog handler?
7. Where did you train, for how long and what did it entail?
8. What additional training have you had? (i.e.) Seminars, conferences, courses, etc.
9. What continual training programs are you on?
10. What associations do you belong to?
11. How many K9 partners have you had?
12. What breed of dog do you use?
13. What is your K9 partner's name?
14. How long have you been together?
15. What duties do you perform?
16. Are you familiar with your dog's sense of smell?
18. Explain your dog's olfactory capabilities.
19. Explain scent.
20. Is a person's scent individual and unique?
21. What does the phrase "reading your dog" mean?
22. What percentage of dog applications involve tracking?
23. How many tracks have you done with your dog?
24. Is your dog trained to discriminate between scents of different people?
25. Do you train in various weather and terrain conditions?
26. Does a person always give off the same scent?
27. Explain the difference between air scent and ground scent.
28. How much street experience does your dog have?
29. How many arrests have you made as a result of successful tracks by your dog?
30. How reliable is your dog on tracks?
31. After how much time delay has your dog been worked to a successful conclusion?
32. On [date of offense] did you use your dog to track?
33. What circumstances brought you to the incident?
34. From what point did you start your track and why?
35. Did you come to a successful conclusion to the track?

Once you have qualified yourself with these questions, go into the details of your tracking application and explain what your conclusions are as a result of the track.

16

16
Police Dog Protection and Safety

Home Safety

One of the locations where officers are least aware of the potential dangers which can injure their dogs is at home. Officers have a tendency to be more relaxed at home and always look after the obvious. It is sometimes the seemingly innocent things that cause injuries to the dog.

Kennel

Location

The kennel at your residence should be in an area fairly secure from the exterior of your property. This will not prevent sabotage, but it will give some security from someone walking up to the kennel. A person seeking revenge or simply targeting you because you are a police officer can easily poison your dog by lobbing a piece of meat over the fence. The dog could also be injured if someone tossed glass into the run or even stabbed at him through the fencing.

When at home he needs to be in a familiar environment, knowing he can be totally relaxed. Even the agitation of people walking close to his run can be stressful to the dog. He needs to be allowed his stress reduction time when off-duty, as much as does the officer. Allowing him to reduce his stress at home makes him less susceptible to injury and mistakes when on shift.

Safety

When the kennel facility is built, the kennel pad must not be set up on the downward slope. Runoff from other sources such as a garage floor could contain potentially toxic substances. The dog should be kenneled in an area that affords him protection from the elements. Any possible trouble the dog could get himself into if left alone for a period of time must be taken into consideration when planning the kennel facility. Seemingly harmless articles can result in tragedy.

Recently an agency lost a dog when it chewed up and ingested carpet left in the kennel for bedding. There is no way one can foresee this type of tragedy, or prevent it from happening at times. However, it is prudent to consider your dog's inclinations when putting items in a kennel area. Think about any possible dangers that may occur, particularly if the dog is a habitual chewer.

It is best to shelter the kennel area with a roof to protect the dog from the elements. Covering the kennel is also a deterrent to passers-by who may be tempted to throw objects over the side of the kennel, regardless of their intent.

Balls

Balls forgotten in the yard by children or left in the kennel can be dangerous, if not made specifically for pets. Tennis balls are fine when being used for water-retrieval training, but that is the only time a dog should have one. Several dogs have lost their lives as a result of choking on such articles by chewing them up and swallowing them, later dying as a result of internal blockage. If children play in the yard where the dog is allowed to roam free on days off, they must be taught not to leave balls out for the dog.

Personal Transport

Dogs do not belong in the open box of a pickup truck. If the dog is transported in a pickup, the dog should be placed in an airline crate that is secured up against the cab of the vehicle. The results of injuries sustained by dogs that have jumped or fallen from an open box truck are traumatic, and the implications are obvious.

When placing the dog in a car that is not made for carrying a dog, such as in a personal vehicle, remove his choke collar. One problem occurred when the choke ring of a service dog got snagged on a seat release in a small station wagon. As the dog tried to move to the other side of the car, the choker tightened. The dog panicked and started to choke as he pulled harder. Luckily the handler saw what was happening and was able to free his partner before any injury occurred.

When in a personal vehicle, the handler is less likely to leave it running with the air conditioning on as he would with a patrol car. Even with windows open for ventilation on a hot day the dog can still get sick and even die from heat stroke.

When lowering windows in a car for ventilation, the officer needs to be aware of the distance. If the dog becomes agitated and starts to bark at passers-by, it is not uncommon for him to get his muzzle close to the opening in the window. Improperly lowered windows leave just enough room to catch one of his canines on the outside edge of the window. The dog's snout can turn to a position where one of his canine teeth get caught and he cannot pull straight back in. In the resulting panic the tooth can snap off. If the officer must open a window for ventilation, he needs to be aware of the dangers of the dog getting one of his canine teeth caught.

Training Hazards

Common sense prevails in most situations. A handler who is keen in his abilities to read and understand his dog's behavior will go a long way in preventing problems. Before entering any training program, an officer must choose the right dog for the job and make sure he is comfortably bonded to him.

> There is never enough said about the importance of bonding with the dog. A proper bond will prevent confusion and potential problems during your training programs.

Equipment must be maintained so it is proper fitting and supple. Oiling harnesses adds to the longevity of harness and prevents unnecessary discomfort for the dog. The harnesses, collars and lines need to be inspected periodically to ensure there are no broken or sharp-edged rivets. A "V" style harness is recommended for on line tracking. Harness with a chest band that goes across the front shoulders can make the dog quite sore – there is a series of nerves very close to the bone which can be irritated by the chest band.

During bite work, decoys need to be cautioned against unnecessary movement of the agitation sleeve, which can injure the dog's mouth. Decoys should be instructed in the proper methods of handling the dog on the sleeve. There is no need to twist the sleeve, shake it up and down, or swing the dog. The dog is worked from the hips and the sleeve level. All agitation equipment such as bite suits and muzzles need to be inspected at each training session for exposed buckles and rivets.

Several companies have been selling new and "improved" bite cuffs that are noted for their durability. These cuffs are jute interlaced with nylon cord to strengthen the material. Avoid this type of cuff. With very little force this cuff can snap the canine teeth out of a German Shepherd. The nylon has no give and it only takes a minor twist to permanently injure the dog.

> Only use cuffs that are made of jute.

Patrol Car Safety

A major concern for dogs during the hot summer months in most North American cities, and year round for agencies in the southern states, is the danger of heat stroke. Frequently we hear of a police dog dying as a result of a lack of air conditioning after the engine on a patrol car fails. Often the dogs are left unattended in the rear of patrol cars while officers attend calls, stop for meal breaks, court, or administrative purposes, or for any number of other reasons. The vehicle is left running, so the dog's compartment can be cooled with the air-conditioning system. As this is a must to keep the dogs healthy on hot days, it is also a potential safety hazard that can quickly kill a dog.

The dog does not have the same capability to cool his body temperature as humans do. When left in a confined area, it is necessary that an adequate cooling system be maintained. The K9 compartment on any car can quickly become a death trap *within minutes* if the cooling system fails and there is inadequate ventilation.

Even moderately hot days can be deadly given the greenhouse effect of the windows of patrol cars. The interior temperature of a car rises due to lack of ventilation, and the dog becomes uncomfortable with the heat. In his agitated attempts to find a source of fresh air he further increases his body temperature, which accelerates the rise in the air temperature of the vehicle. Within ten minutes of engine failure in moderate heat the dog can be dead.

Window Tinting

Window tinting, using a titanium alloy, is effective in helping to cut down the heat to the rear compartment on a car. Titanium alloy reflects large portions of the sun's heat while allowing a lighter tint on the windows.

Tinting patrol car windows is recommended for two reasons: first, for the benefits of heat reduction in the dog's compartment, and second, to give the dog some limited "privacy." People are less likely to notice the dog in the car, especially at night.

People often wander over to a K9 car when it is unoccupied by the officer and tease the dog. This results in unnecessary agitation for the dog and can result in injury. Dogs have sustained chipped canines from biting at the glass of the patrol car while being teased by drunks who tap on the windows. The frequency of this type of occurrence is less when the windows on the car are darkened to some degree.

Monitoring Device

Radiotronics Inc. provides a state-of-the-art electronic device that constantly monitors the status of the patrol car. The system, known as *K9 Lifeguard,* provides protection for the dog when he is left unattended in the back of the patrol car. This device was engineered to provide foolproof protection for the dog.

The system is very well designed. Thought has even gone into the possibility that the dog might accidentally bump the switches to the unit off, effectively turning off his source of protection. To prevent such an occurrence the unit is built using aircraft switches designed to be pulled out before they can be activated.

Lifeguard mounts under the dash of the patrol unit and continuously monitors the mechanical performance of the engine and the interior temperature of the car with electronic sensors. Should the engine fail, or the temperature suddenly rise due to an air conditioning failure, the system immediately detects the fault and alerts the handler by a variety of methods. The vehicle's horn and siren, as well as the emergency lights, are activated.

There is an optional pager that can be worn by the officer if he is in a building, out of earshot of his vehicle. Another optional feature enables the system to automatically roll down the windows of the patrol unit, if equipped for this.

The *Lifeguard* system is maintenance-free. It is constantly in operation and the officer never has to remember to turn it on once it is mounted. The system becomes an integral part of the vehicle's operating system, twenty-four hours a day. There are built-in failure systems as well, to prevent accidental activation of the system. For example, if the car stalls at a stop light a warning tone sounds before activation of the unit's alarm system, to permit the officer time to shut the unit off before it activates.

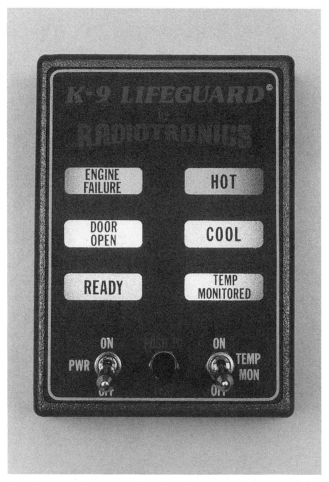

Another vital piece of technology manufactured by Radiotronics is the K9 Lifeguard temperature monitoring system.

K9 Body Armor

Second Chance Body Armor has recently tested a vest they specifically designed for K9 operations. The vest ensures maximum comfort for the dog, and allows him to move naturally, without restriction. Care has been taken to make sure there is nothing on the vest that will get hung up on obstructions the dog might run across during a building search. The dog needs to learn how to work with the vest on if it is going to be used on him during deployments. Training should be done to condition the dog to wearing it. This item should become a standard piece of equipment for any K9 unit.

17

17
K9 Trauma Care

Preparation and Training

Proper preparation and training can effectively change the outcome of traumatic injuries that your dog may encounter in the field. The treatments outlined in this chapter are only a guide and in no way should be considered complete. In all cases consult your veterinarian for follow-up treatment.

As the job becomes more diverse, more dogs suffer injuries as a direct result of confrontations with suspects and from hazards in the field. Dogs come up against everything from broken glass to bullets. Proper application of effective first aid can often alleviate the problem so no further treatment is required. In drastic cases, the proper use of your first aid knowledge and equipment can often save the life of your partner.

Every K9 officer should attend an extended trauma care program developed specifically for police K9. At the very least, have a basic K9 first aid program developed and presented by your veterinarian. Programs are available with instruction about advanced life support for police dogs. These programs explain extended emergency care and cover intubation techniques, starting I.V.s and the proper use of various injectable drugs. This training is used effectively in the field to save the lives of valuable service dogs. Co-ordination with your local paramedics and emergency medical technicians can provide you with a team effectively prepared to deal with serious canine injuries.

Case Study

In Washington State, Officer Randy Gehrke lost his dog when it was shot numerous times in the face with a small calibre handgun. Although all attempts to revive the dog were futile, the efforts that went into the situation were extensive. Paramedics were called to the scene and were patched via radio to the department's veterinarian. The dog was intubated and CPR was started immediately by the handler and the medics. I.V.'s were started to keep the dog's pressure up and appropriate drugs were administered. Attempts were made to start the dogs heart using a defibrillator.

All efforts were made by the paramedics and the dog handler, co-ordinated through radio communication by the veterinarian. The dog did not survive and an autopsy revealed that all four shots had to be considered fatal injuries.

Of note, the dog did manage to stay on the suspect and keep him off balance until the fifth shot was fired. Even after receiving four wounds that he would soon die from, the dog continued to fight. This continued fight caused the suspect to accidentally shoot himself in the head in his panic to escape. He too later died in hospital.

This is one example of the extent of efficiency that can be attained with a team of people who are open to new ideas and are willing to get involved in programs. If you take the time to implement such a program you may find that it is never used. If you do need it, you will be forever grateful that you took the time to put together an effective program.

Emergency Care

Emergency care of your dog is basically common sense. If you follow the same basic rules that apply to the treatment of people, you will have a good concept of what is required of you in assisting your canine. One concept that is different in the trauma care of a dog is that you must be able to adequately determine the extent of the injuries. Unlike people, your dog cannot tell you where it hurts or how he feels. You must be thorough enough in your examination to determine your dog's injuries, in order to ascertain how you are going to deal with them.

Vital Signs

Normal heart rate ranges between 80 to 140 beats per minute for a dog. Place your hands on the chest just behind the elbow, positioning your hands around the chest wall, and press gently until you can determine the heart rate (method: count the hearbeats over a period of 15 seconds and multiply by four).

Your dog's normal body temperature is between 38 degrees C (100.5 degrees F) and 39.2 degrees C (102.5 degrees F). The dog's ability to withstand fevers is not as flexible as that of the human body. As such, great care must be taken to ensure that any fever is treated rapidly and effectively.

Dogs are highly susceptible to heat stroke and to that end, agitation sessions on hot days should be carefully monitored to be sure the dog does not get sick. High fever in the dog can result in brain damage in a very short time and even death if treatment is not expeditious.

Temperature strips are available that can be placed easily in the dog's flank to obtain a temperature reading. The strip is color-coded and will indicate the dog's temperature by a color change. Basal body temperature is the most accurate and obtained rectally. Apply a surgical lubricant to the bulb of a rectal thermometer and gently insert about two inches into the rectum. If the dog is active you will need to effectively restrict him for about 90 seconds while the reading is being taken.

A dog's respiration can be monitored by placing a hand on the dog's chest and checking for the rise and fall. If the dog is not breathing, or if he has under ten respirations per minute, an injection of Dopram may help.

Procedure For K9 Resuscitation

1. First, be certain the dog is not breathing on his own.

2. Check the mouth and nose area for any mucous, foreign materials or objects. Wipe the area clean and remove any material you find.
3. Pull the dog's tongue forward to clear the airway and tip his head slightly upwards from his body. Use a piece of gauze or material in your hand to make it easier to maintain a hold on the dog's tongue.
5. Place your mouth over the dog's nose and blow. Check to be sure the dog's chest rises as you perform the respirations. If the dog's chest does not rise, check for airway obstructions. Be sure the tongue is pulled forward and the head is tilted slightly back.
6. Continue to repeat the procedure to allow the air to exit. Respirations should be maintained between 15 and 20 breaths per minute.

Heimlich Manoeuvre

The Heimlich manoeuvre is an emergency procedure used to dislodge any obstruction in the dog's airway.

1. Pull your dog up against you and interlock your fingers around the dog's upper abdomen in the hollow just under the rib cage area. If the dog is too large to manoeuvre in this manner, lay the animal on a firm surface.
2. Place one hand on top of the other, with the heel of the bottom hand pressed into the middle of the abdomen immediately below the rib cage. Forcibly push or pull upward one or more times to dislodge the obstruction.
3. If the object is visible, have someone else try to hold the dog's tongue and lower jaw and remove the article with your fingers, or forceps if available. If you are successful in removing the foreign object and the dog does not resume breathing, immediately start mouth-to-nose respirations.

Transporting An Injured Dog

In preparing the dog for transport, remember that he may be out of character if injured and afraid. He may strike out and bite in such situations and must be approached accordingly.
- If necessary apply a muzzle before doing any first aid or trying to transport him.
- Keep the dog calm while preparing to move him.
- Soothing him by stroking him and talking to him will go a long way in keeping him still while making preparations.

Backboards

Adopt the use of a backboard for K9 units. Backboards are easily made to size for a dog and secured in the trunk area of your patrol unit for emergencies. If you do not have a K9 backboard available to you, if the situation warrants, have an ambulance attend your location and make use of a backboard from their unit. If necessary have them transport as well. As discussed earlier, good co-ordination with the emergency medical personnel in your area can be very beneficial when your dog is down.

Secure the dog on the backboard and if at all possible, cover the board with a blanket first to make it more comfortable and less slippery for the dog. This also helps to make it easier to move the dog if needed. The blanket itself can be used as a makeshift stretcher by laying the dog on the blanket and rolling the edges up to the dog on each side. The rolled up ends can be used as handles to lift the dog. This method can be used to carry the dog to the backboard, or to unload the dog from a backboard onto the vet's table.

Shock

Shock is a critical medical condition brought on by heavy trauma such as gunshot wounds, knife attacks or blunt trauma injuries. It can also result from dehydration during heat stroke, such as when the dog is left in a sealed car. It is characterized in the dog by:

- lowered body temperature
- uncontrollable shivering
- a distinct loss of pink coloring in the gums.

Shock is the body's method of using blood flow from peripheral tissue to support the major organs in emergencies. This results in a serious restriction in the delivery of oxygen and nutrients to tissues, as well as in the removal of cellular waste. Circulatory shock has various classifications depending on the cause, however Hypovolemic shock is the problem that we as K9 officers will be required to deal with on the street.

Hypovolemic shock is the type of shock you will deal with in gunshot or stab wounds or traumatic incidents. A rapid decrease in blood volume as a result of traumatic injury is the single most common cause of shock. It results from loss of blood through internal and external bleeding, by dehydration and also through fluid losses such as blood plasma that seeps from large burn areas.

Symptoms

Symptoms of Hypovolemic shock are:
- a distinct pallor of the dog's gums
- lowered blood pressure
- dilation of the pupils
- heavy, rapid breathing

Kidney failure may result due to a lack of renal blood flow. This results from decreased renal blood flow and in turn lowers urine production.

Treatment

Treatment is to rehydrate the dog as soon as possible via the administration of intravenous fluid, if the situation is severe. Initial treatment is to keep the dog warm and calm. Wrap the dog in a blanket and if available, supplement with hot water bottles. Treat any other conditions as prescribed and transport as soon as possible.

Shock is a potentially fatal condition and no time should be wasted in getting the dog the appropriate medical attention at your nearest emergency animal hospital.

If you find yourself in the field and you have had appropriate training, you may be able to use adrenaline stimulants prescribed by your veteranarian and kept in your trauma kit to assist the dog's heart.

Poisoning

Signs of poisoning vary, depending on the type of substance your dog has ingested. If you suspect your dog has consumed some form of poisonous substance, contact your veterinarian immediately. A poison control centre can also provide valuable information as to what steps to take.

Symptoms

Symptoms of poisoning may include:
- uncontrollable twitching of the skin
- agitation or nervousness
- heavy panting
- excessive salivation
- diarrhea and vomiting

Often there is difficulty in breathing. In some cases the pupils will be dilated, in others constricted.

Treatment

Treatment is often identical to treatment that would be given humans in similar circumstances.

> Do not treat your dog without consultation, as you may cause more injury if you provide the wrong antidotes.

Antifreeze

The substance ethylene glycol is found in many products, such as antifreeze and windshield de-icer products. This is one of the most common poisons and is highly dangerous. It is highly palatable to a dog, which makes it more dangerous than most poisons – the antifreeze tastes sweet to a dog, and they have a tendency to ingest large quantities of the product if it is available.

Symptoms

Symptoms of antifreeze ingestion are:
- disorientation
- vomiting
- collapse
- eventually death.

Treatment

Should you encounter a situation where your dog has ingested any quantity of antifreeze at all, induce vomiting with apomorphine and transport him to your veterinarian without delay.

Insecticide

Another common type of poison that the patrol dog is likely to come into contact with is insecticides. Products such as fly bait, carbamates, organophosphates and rat poisons are a few of the insecticides to be concerned with. Symptoms of insecticide poisoning include excessive salivation, muscle tremors or convulsions, staggering, vomiting and diarrhea, heavy panting and constricted pupils. The dog will eventually fall unconscious and into a coma.

Treatment for insecticides includes 31 grams (1 ounce) of water given orally, followed by a 3cc injection of Atropine. If your dog is under 27 kg (60 pounds), reduce the atropine to 2cc. If the dog is staggering or has gone into convulsions, 2cc of Valium can be administered. Should the dog stop breathing or his respirations fall below 10 per minute, 2cc of Dopram should be administered. All medications injected can be given intravenously, intramuscularly, or subcutaneously.

Rat Poison

Rat poison is one of the more common poisons encountered on the street, particularly in the coastal areas and shipyards. Rat poisons cause hemorrhaging and are extremely dangerous. Vitamin K and prompt action by your veterinarian are vital. Induce vomiting and contact your vet immediately.

Explosive Materials

All explosive materials are toxic to some degree and should be treated as highly dangerous to your dog. The symptoms of poisoning in the dog that has ingested an explosive substance include:
- breathing difficulties
- vomiting
- diarrhea
- a blue tinge to the gums
- falls into convulsions and if not treated will die.

Advanced toxicity in the dog is indicated by:
- stomach irritations
- hepatitis
- anemia
- dermatitis
- urinary infections
- cardiac irregularities.

In such cases the dog's life might not be immediately threatened, but he is in danger and urgent treatment is required. This is usually indicative of a build up of toxic substances in the dog's system.

Smokeless powder without Nitroglycerin is non-toxic and can be treated by inducing vomiting in the dog. Transport to your veterinarian for further treatment.

Smokeless powder with Nitroglycerin, TNT, and dynamite are all nitrate poisons.

Treatment

Induce vomiting in the dog and treat with large doses of activated charcoal. Your veterinarian will be able to administer a 2 percent solution of methylene at a rate of 1 ml for every 2.2 kg (5 pounds) of body weight. Follow up treatment with a special diet that includes high calcium content and the administration of vitamins A and D.

C4 Explosive has a unique set of symptoms over and above those indicated by nitrates. The dog will be hyperactive and show bizarre behavior changes. Treatment is the same as nitrates, but an injection of Valium is also prescribed.

Narcotics

Drug-detection dogs have more exposure to potential deadly chemicals than most other dogs. They routinely detect and recover substances that are harmful. The locations of the searches alone can pose perils that are not often a part of the patrol team's repertoire. The substances are often in powdered forms, easy for the dog to ingest. For example, a search in a residence where drugs are produced can expose the dog not only to the finished product, but also to the various chemicals used for production.

Stimulants are one area of concern for drug-detection dogs. Amphetamines, LSD, cocaine and marijuana are all potentially hazardous for the dog. Most narcotics dogs are trained with an aggressive find. During such a search the dog can quite easily come in contact with the object of his search and death can be swift if any of the product is ingested or infused via the skin.

Narcotic Treatment Specifics

Marijuana

- Causes an increased heart rate, decreased blood pressure and lethargy. The dog may vomit, be unsteady on his feet, and have seizures.

Treatment

- Induce vomiting.
- Administer activated charcoal.
- Transport to your veterinarian for further assistance.

Amphetamines

Amphetamines cause the dog to be restless and hyperactive. The pupils will be dilated and he may experience tremors and become "shocky." The heart rate will be sporadic and the circulatory system may fail.

Treatment

- Administer activated charcoal.
- Sedatives such as valium may need to be administered. If you have been trained in the proper trauma care techniques, you can administer 1 milligram of Valium for every kilogram (2.2 pounds) of body weight of the dog, to a maximum of 20 milligrams.
- Transport to your veterinarian.

Cocaine

Cocaine causes dilated pupils, tremors, shivering, profuse salivation, vomiting and increased body temperature in the dog. He may go into convulsions.

Treatment

- Induce vomiting and administer activated charcoal.
- Valium can be administered to control seizures.
- Respiratory failure is common and endotracheal intubation supported by a resuscitation system is often needed to keep the dog breathing.
- Transport to your veterinarian as soon as possible.

Heroin

The dog will experience drowsiness, become lethargic, be unco-ordinated and have a decreased sensitivity to pain. Vomiting may occur. As the poison advances, the dog may go into a delerium, resulting in convulsions and a coma.

Treatment

- Induce vomiting.
- Introduce activated charcoal and transport urgently.
- The dog's most likely cause of death will be from respiratory failure, and the proper application of resuscitation techniques can greatly improve his chances of survival. Narcan or Naloxone can be administered at .01 to .02 milligrams per kilogram (2.2 pounds) of body weight.
- Valium may also need to be administered to control seizures.
- Respiratory support may be required during transport.

> These procedures should not be attempted without proper instruction and follow-up training by a qualified veterinarian or K9 trauma care specialist. Once you have learned these techniques your chances of saving your dog from a narcotics overdose are good.

General Guidelines on Poisoning

Try to find out what type of product has been ingested. Once you have determined the type of poison, there are several emergency procedures that will assist you in treating your dog. In all cases you need to rush your dog to your veterinarian as soon as possible. Proper care given at the roadside, however, can enhance your dog's chances of survival.

1. Care begins with the proper determination of what poison has been ingested. Your best source of information is always the label on the poison packaging.

2. Call your veterinarian or poison control centre immediately and advise them of your situation. Have the name of the ingested product available.
3. To treat the dog with liquids, I advise using a syringe or basting tube. Give liquid only if your dog is still alert and functioning in a capacity where he can swallow without choking. Tilt the dog's head back and keep his head elevated. You can form a pocket in which to inject the liquid by pulling the corner of the lip away from the jaw. Stroke the dog's throat to encourage him to swallow, in the same manner as you do when you administer pills.
5. If vomiting is required, place an APOMORPHINE tablet under the lower eyelid of the dog. APOMORPHINE is quickly absorbed into the dog's system and will induce vomiting. It usually works faster and more effectively than hydrogen peroxide mixtures or syrup of Ipecac and is far easier to administer.

> Vomiting should not be induced if the product ingested by the dog is acid, alkali, or petroleum-based.

Products such as strychnine, gasoline, paint thinners and cleaning fluids all fall into this category. Inducing vomiting will only cause more damage to the dog.

In such cases milk is given to soothe the tissues, and administration of powdered, activated charcoal may be applicable. This is a simple yet effective remedy in situations where there is not a remedy available that is specific to the poison and it is not advisable to induce vomiting. The activated charcoal, once ingested, soaks up the poisonous materials and neutralizes the stomach contents. The poison is then carried through the digestive tract, trapped by the charcoal and safely excreted by the dog. This treatment can effectively prevent much of the poison from damaging tissue or entering the dog's system.

POISON INFORMATION CHART

POISON	INDUCE VOMITING?	POISON	INDUCE VOMITING?
Acetone	Yes	Crayons	Yes
Alkali	No	Diazonon	Yes
Alcohol	Yes	Dichlorvos	Yes
Amphetamine	Yes	Fertilizers	No
Antifreeze	Yes	Heroin	Yes
Ant Bait	Yes	House Plants	Yes
Arsenic	Yes	Insecticide	Yes
Bleach	No	Lead	Yes
Burnt Lime	No	Lye	No
Chemicals	No	Malathion	Yes
Cleaners	No	Pine Oil	Yes
Cocaine	Yes	Rat Poison	Yes

> In all cases it is vital that you transport the dog to your veterinarian immediately.

If you have been trained by your veterinarian to give injections in the field, you will be advised as to the amount of antidote to deliver.

> Apomorphine, valium, dopram, naline, narcan or any other injectable medication should *not* be given without appropriate training, and only in the amounts prescribed by your veterinarian.

Torsion

Torsion is a common ailment in the larger breeds of dogs and quite a common occurrence in police service dogs. Also known as "Bloat," this medical problem comes on fast and is very deadly. For unknown reasons the stomach of the dog goes into spasm and turns, effectively closing off the entrance from the esophagus and the exit into the intestinal tract. The gases within the stomach expand rapidly, causing the blood flow to the stomach tissues to be restricted. Gangrene sets in rapidly and the dog is usually dead within hours.

Torsion can be recognized by a bloated distended midsection. Early symptoms include:

- vomiting
- diarrhea
- tenderness in the stomach area.

As the problem advances the dog will be in excruciating pain, and will not be able to hold anything down. Sometimes he will drag his body along the ground in an attempt to alleviate the pain.

Treatment

Immediate pressure release from the internal gases followed by immediate surgery, are required. It is important that the handler be able to recognize this problem as the onset is very fast. The problem occurs frequently after feedings, even if the dog is relaxed. There seems to be frequent occurrences where the dog is overheated from exercise and then consumes a large quantity of cold water. It is a good idea to keep an eye on the dog for an hour or so after feeding, as this problem usually occurs at this time. Although it is not known for sure what causes the stomach to spasm, these are instances that may cause an onset of torsion. Smaller feedings twice a day, or restricting feedings to the end of a work shift seem to be helpful, but will not prevent it from occurring. It is not recommended to give the dog a heavy meal before going on shift or putting him through a series of strenuous exercises.

Immediate veterinary intervention is required if the dog is to be saved. If the dog is lucky enough to have surgery before the tissue is damaged, the surgeon will staple the stomach into a position that will prevent a recurrence of the problem.

Fractures And Dislocations

With the number of fences dog teams come across and the various circumstances they find themselves in, it is not unlikely to encounter a situation which results in the dog fracturing his leg.

> Keep the dog calm and treat by immobilizing the limb before transporting him.

In these circumstances the dog may become hostile during attempts to help him, as it will be quite painful for him.

Treatment

- Before starting treatment, it is advisable to muzzle him to prevent him from injuring you or anyone else that might try to assist.
- As in other traumatic injuries he must be treated for shock.
- Once the injured limb has been splinted, apply a cold ice pack to reduce swelling and pain.
- Transport on a backboard once he is properly secured.

Knife And Gunshot Wounds

Surprisingly enough, many dogs survive gunshot wounds. One of the mindsets people have after being shot is that they will die. Death has resulted from the ensuing shock brought on by the person's fears and mental condition at the time of injury. In some cases it was proven that the wounds received by an individual were in fact not lethal, yet the victim died. Although a dog has fear of getting hurt and obviously reacts to pain, he has no concept or fear of death. Many dogs that have been shot have continued to pursue suspects and successfully apprehend them.

Treatment

As in the treatment of people, the number one priority is to maintain an airway in the dog and to stop bleeding. Direct pressure applied with military shell dressings or other large compresses is very effective. A most effective compress that can be kept in a K9 trauma kit for just such an emergency is menstrual pads (Kotex or some other such brand).

Treat the dog for shock (loss of blood can rapidly bring on shock and death). Keep him as quiet as possible and transport him as quickly as possible. If the compress gets soaked through with blood, do not remove it to replace it. Simply place more compresses on top of the original. This allows whatever coagulation that has begun to remain in place.

There are various injections that can be given to assist in getting the blood to coagulate more efficiently. This should only be done under the direct supervision of a veterinarian, or by an officer who has received an advanced life support program for K9.

Knife attacks are treated in a manner similar to gunshot wounds. If the knife has been left in the animal, care must be taken to prevent the dog from moving, and the weapon should not be touched. Pack around the weapon at the point of entry and apply enough pressure to shut down bleeding. Transport only after you have secured the dog to a backboard in a manner that will prevent him from moving around.

Blood Typing

It is advisable to start a program with your veterinarian to prepare for potential injuries that may involve internal or external blood loss. Make an appointment with your department vet and make arrangements for each dog to be blood typed.

Have blood drawn and stored for future emergencies. Although blood matching is not as critical in canines as it is in humans, it is beneficial to have a steady supply of your own dog's blood products available should it be required. By matching all the dogs in your section, the vet can then use the appropriate match from the resources you have prepared.

Blunt Trauma

This type of injury can often cause internal bleeding. The dog will show signs of discomfort and possibly a puffy stomach. His breathing will be rapid and he will have a weak pulse. The gums will show signs of shock by appearing to have a blue tinge or pallor to them.

Treatment

There is nothing you can immediately do in this type of situation. Treat for shock and transport to your veterinarian quickly.

Snake Bite

Most attacks will result in two puncture wounds accompanied by extreme swelling and pain in the immediate area of the bite.

Treatment

Rapid treatment is vital to save the dog's life. Obtain a snake bite kit from a veterinarian that counteracts the types of snakes in your area. If the dog is bitten and you cannot transport him immediately to your vet, apply a tourniquet between the bite area and the heart if the bite is on any of his legs. Restrain your dog to prevent any unnecessary movement and keep him as calm as possible to help keep his heart rate low.

If you have been trained by your veterinarian, use the supplied snake-bite kit as instructed by your veterinarian. If you do not have a kit available, try to make a cut between the puncture wounds and induce bleeding in an attempt to wash poison out of the wound site. Transport as soon as possible.

Heat Stroke

This is the most frequent problem with service dogs. Heat stroke is most common as the result of a dog left in a vehicle on a hot day. The dog's temperature starts to rise and as he becomes more uncomfortable he will start to move around and look for an opening for fresh air. As he becomes more agitated his body temperature begins to rise faster. He will start to lick the glass and eventually paw and bite at the glass in his attempts to free himself of the vehicle. Eventually the dog will become unco-ordinated and collapse into unconsciousness. In minutes he will die.

When doing bite work with a dog be sure the dog does not become overheated. Monitor the dog carefully. Give him an adequate supply of water and keep the training sessions short if working on a particularly hot day. It is best to give him a quick spray down with a hose periodically, which helps keep his temperature low.

Should you find your dog unconscious with a high body temperature, or drooling, vomiting, or in near collapse with heavy panting, remove him immediately to a cool shady area. Pour copious amounts of cold water on him and bathe him thoroughly, ensuring that you get through the underdown of the coat. Use water-soaked gauze pads to soak his gums and keep them moist.

Once your dog regains consciousness, or if he is conscious, allow him to drink water. Fast rapid cooling is effective and usually, if caught in time, the dog will show no after affects. Transport to your veterinarian for a routine medical check.

18

18
Valor

Officers' Roll Of Valor

The following three dog handlers, two of whom I met, died as a result of gunshot wounds sustained during K9 applications. Through the generous support and assistance of their families, I was able to add this section to the book.

I had an opportunity to compete with Fred House in police dog championships. His skills as a handler and quick wit will always be how his fellow officers remember him. While preparing this manual I had the opportunity to speak with his brother Tom, who understood my cause and assisted me in compiling information on Fred. I also had the pleasure of speaking with the parents of Michael Buday, as well as Jim Hansen's family. They too were generous and helpful in supplying me with the needed documentation and photos.

It was not an easy decision for any of the families and during some of the conversations tears were shed as we brought back memories long suppressed. I hope every officer who reads this book remembers and appreciates the contribution these men and their families have made.

Constable Michael Buday – Royal Canadian Mounted Police

Constable Michael Buday, a dog handler with the Royal Canadian Mounted Police, was shot in the neck and killed on Teslin Lake in British Columbia on March 19, 1985. At the time of his death, he was involved in a wilderness search for a burglary suspect.

The killer, a Michael Oros, had lived in the northern regions of Canada for several years. He proclaimed himself a prophet and a Vietnam veteran. He was known for his violent outbreaks and was suspected in the disappearance of a trapper in 1981. Oros became a burglary suspect when a Whitehorse family discovered their cabin broken into. An RCMP-directed aircraft flew over the remote lake area to search for Oros. Once he knew they had spotted him, he shot at the aircraft but missed. The police flew back to Teslin, where more officers were recruited to confront Oros on the following day.

Constable Buday, the team's dog handler, and twelve other officers dropped into the area. Oros, an experienced woodsman armed with two rifles, surprised them from the rear. He opened fire without warning, shooting Constable Buday before being killed by the return fire of the other officers.

Constable Michael Buday – Royal Canadian Mounted Police

Lt. Fred F. House – Utah State Department Of Corrections

Lt. Fred House, an officer with the Utah State Department of Corrections, was killed in the line of duty on January 28, 1988. He was participating in the tactical resolution of a thirteen day standoff between law enforcement and a group of radical fundamentalists who had heavily armed and then barricaded themselves into a fortified structure after bombing a church in Summit County, Utah.

Lt. Fred House – Utah State Department of Corrections

Officer Jim Hanson – Anchorage Police Department

On July 17, 1986, Officer Hanson, a K9 Officer with the Anchorage Police Department, responded to a call involving a bank robbery suspect who had shot at an officer. While backing up a second K9 Officer who was tracking the suspect, Officer Hanson was shot and killed as he followed the dog into the suspect's location. The suspect was subsequently shot several times by other officers, but managed to survive.

Officer Harry B. (Jim) Hanson – Anchorage Police Department

K9 Honor Roll

Following is a collection of various incidents I have gathered over the years in my research into K9-involved incidents. These show the valor and courage of the K9 officers and their four-legged partners. I include these incidents to stress the realities of the job and to honor those dogs that have died in the line of duty. I do not know who wrote the following poem, but I know that it holds true for the police service dog.

The Working Dog

My eyes are your eyes to watch and protect yours.
My ears are your ears to hear and detect evil minds in the dark.
My nose is your nose to scent the invader of your domain.
And so you may live, my life is also yours.

K9 Valiant – Vancouver, BC, 1967

At 8:45 a.m. on December 18, 1967, Constable Mike Wellman and his dog Valiant of the Vancouver Police Dog Squad, were dispatched to an apartment at 1460 Nelson St. to assist in the apprehension of a prison escapee who had stated that he would not be taken alive.

The wanted man, Joseph McKenna, 32, was known to be armed. He had been serving a life sentence for murder after shooting a man four times in a nightclub argument. Police had received information of the escapee's location and had surrounded the apartment. Officers at the scene called for the man to surrender and kicked open the door. They were answered by two shots fired from a bedroom. The shots entered a doorjamb inches from the officers. Police fired a shotgun blast into the room. Immediately Police Dog Valiant was released and bounded into the room after the gunman. The man was hiding under a bed and, as the dog pounced, he fired a shot which caused Valiant to yelp with pain.

Wellman called the dog to heel and obediently Valiant retunred to his master and sat waiting for the next command. Police again called on McKenna to surrender. He called out that he was giving up and did so meekly. He later told police that he would never have surrendered if it wasn't for the fact that he was scared the dog would come in again. Police at the scene were not immediately aware that the dog had been shot. Valiant's thick coat hid the bullet wound and there was not much external bleeding.

As the prisoner was being taken out to a police car, Valiant stood guard and it was then that Wellman noticed his dog was bleeding from the stomach. He was rushed to a veterinary hospital but the wound was serious, having punctured a lung, liver, kidney and intestime. Valiant died of his injuries after a three-hour operation.

In 1967, the *Vancouver Sun* presented its "Award of Merit" posthumously to Valiant for the most outstanding dog case of the year.

K9 Justin – Vancouver, BC 1976

Police Dog Justin died May 11, 1976, after responding to a "shots fired" call. With his handler Constable Gary Foster nearby, Justin flushed the man, Gordon Rudyk, from the bushes at East 2nd Avenue and Garden. The suspect, who left his shotgun behind, ran across the park and Justin was ordered to apprehend him. Justin caught the suspect and took hold of him as he had been trained to do. He was stabbed repeatedly before police officers could assist. The suspect was arrested but not before Constable Foster was himself cut by Rudyk. Justin, mortally wounded, was rushed to a veterinary hospital. He died during surgery.

Justin was awarded the Catherine Price Gold Medal by the SPCA for his dedication to duty. He was also presented with the *Vancouver Sun* 1976 "Award of Merit."

K9 Zeiko – New Orleans, 1981

On October 15, 1981 a New Orleans service dog was shot in the face after tracking two armed suspects wanted for car theft. K9 Zeiko, a male Rottweiler, tracked the suspects to a hiding place under a house and in the subsequent shootout with police, one suspect killed and the other was taken into custody after receiving a gunshot wound to the leg.

K9 Rebel – Prince Georges, 1984

On October 27, 1984 an 18-year-old Washington man was shot and killed by a Prince Georges County police officer after he broke into a school and fatally stabbed the officer's dog. The incident occurred in a junior high school in the early hours of the morning. Officer Ewing and K9 Rebel attended the school in response to a silent alarm.

The dog searched the building and located two suspects in a dark room near the auditorium, one male and one female. The male subject attacked the dog with a knife, stabbing him twice in the chest. He then came towards the officer. The officer shot the suspect with two shots to the chest as the suspect advanced, killing him.

K9 Rebel was a 3 1/2 year-old German Shepherd and had been in service for two years at the time of his death.

K9 Sony – Ventura, CA, 1984

In the morning hours of August 26, 1984 a kidnapping occurred in Ventura, California. Police located the suspect and the victim in a vehicle, and the suspect pushed the victim out of his car and a police pursuit ensued. Officers chased the suspect until he jumped out of his vehicle and ran into a mobile home park. Officer Alstot gave chase on foot with his service dog Sony.

The suspect threatened suicide by placing a gun to his head and then he started pointing the weapon at the officers. The suspect continued to weave in and out of the mobile homes, pointing the weapon at the officers each time he came into sight. Due to the surrounding area and the citizens watching nearby the officers were unable to use deadly force for fear of an innocent citizen getting hurt. By this time they had closed in on the suspect and as the suspect turned his back on the officers, Alstot gave Sony his command to attack and sent him after the suspect.

As Sony got a few feet away from taking down the suspect, the suspect turned around and saw the dog. He fired two rounds at point blank range into Sony's head. After the shots were fired the suspect dropped his weapon and put his hands on top of his head. Sony was killed instantly. K9 Sony was awarded a Memorial Award from the American Police Hall of Fame for giving his life while helping and trying to protect his handler during the apprehension of a criminal.

K9 Ward – Lewis County, WA, 1985

On October 15, 1985, at about 00:46 hours, while on the track of a suspect fleeing from a burglary of a local high school, K9 Ward died as a result of a single stab wound to the chest. An 18-year-old white male suspect, armed with a handgun and a knife, was apprehended one hour later in the area. Ward was a five-year-old German Shepherd. He had been with the Sheriff's office for about ten months and in that time was involved in 35 to 40 felony arrests.

K9 Gero – Gainesville, FL, 1986

On October 3, 1986, a report of a burglary in progress was reported to the Gainesville, Florida Police Department. Officer Mike Pruitt responded with his K9 partner Gero as patrol teams surrounded the building and contained the perimeter. As Officer Pruitt entered the building, the suspect opened fire with a large calibre handgun, striking K9 Gero in the shoulder. Gero, although wounded continued his attack and grabbed the suspect. The suspect fired again at point blank range. This time the force of the blast from the weapon knocked the dog backwards, allowing the gunman to turn his weapon on Officer Pruitt. Gero again managed to gather the strength to attack and lunged between the officer and the suspect in time to take a third bullet.

This action allowed Pruitt and Officer Baker enough time to effectively return fire, neutralizing the suspect. K9 Gero was dead on the scene.

K9 Murph – Tempe, AZ, 1986

On November 21, 1986 a suspect shot a Scottsdale police officer and fled in a stolen car. Numerous citizens were also injured by the suspect. The suspect was pursued through the streets of Tempe, and shots fired by the suspect during the chase struck the pursuing police cars. During the chase the suspect grabbed a six-year-old child off the street, using him as a hostage, and broke into a nearby home where he barricaded himself with the young boy.

SWAT team members showed up at the scene and entered the dark house in an attempt to rescue the boy. During the initial entry the suspect opened fire on the officers, however they refused initially to return fire as they could not see where the boy was in the darkness. As the gunfire erupted Sgt. Ralph Tranter was struck in the face with a Glazer .44 magnum round when he entered the house. Despite the wound in his right eye, Sgt. Tranter managed to find the young boy and rescue him, running out of the residence with the boy in his arms as the gun battle continued in the residence.

As soon as Tranter was clear Officer Carlos Araiza sent his K9 partner Murph into the house from the back entranceway to engage the suspect as another team of tactical officers broke through the barricaded front entrance. As Murph encountered the suspect he was shot and killed. This action, however, bought enough time for officers Les Gray, Gary Lindberg and Tom Stubbs to enter the residence from the front. A few moments later Officer Gray encountered the suspect, who was crouching down with a .44 magnum Bulldog revolver in one hand and a .357 magnum revolver in the other.

The suspect opened fire on Officer Gray, striking him in the right hand and bicep. Officer Gray pulled back momentarily, then returned fire with his shotgun, striking the suspect in the chest and killing him instantly.

K9 Murph joined the Tempe Police Department in February 1981 and was assigned to Officer Araiza. During their time together they received eight departmental commendations.

K9 Bear – Illinois State Police, 1987

Illinois State Police K9 Bear was shot to death on October 4, 1987, after being sent into a cornfield in an attempt to subdue a man wanted in connection with the wounding of four people. Sgt. Jim Buysee and K9 Bear located the suspect during the search and upon approach, Bear was shot by the suspect. The suspect then took his own life. K9 Bear was five years old at the time of his death.

K9 Ando – Indianapolis, IA, 1988

In 1988 a police dog jumped into the path of a shotgun blast, saving the life of a deputy sheriff. The German Shepherd, named Ando, had worked with Cpl. Paul Thompson for about two years before the shootout. Thompson was involved in a stand-off with a man who barricaded himself inside a house after a traffic accident. The man charged Thompson, firing a shotgun blast at pointblank range. The dog jumped at the suspect, taking the brunt of the blast, and was killed instantly. The deputy received gunshot wounds to the foot and the suspect managed to escape.

Officer Randy Gehrke and K9 Zach

K9 Zach – King County, WA, 1988

On July 6, 1988, at 19:00 hours, Southwest Patrol (Burien Area) was dispatched to a forgery investigation at the Marriott Hotel, located near the SeaTac Airport. As officers arrived the suspect saw them and fled on foot to a waiting vehicle with a 17-year-old female inside. The suspect took off at high speed in the stolen BMW and a pursuit ensued. The pursuit lasted five minutes and ended when the suspect mistakenly took a wrong turn into a Washington State Patrol office.

He and the female fled on foot and the troopers saw the female hand a small black object to the male suspect which later turned out to be a .25 calibre semiautomatic pistol. The female was caught by one of the troopers and the other trooper chased the male suspect into a very heavily wooded and brushy ravine where he lost sight of the suspect.

A tight perimeter was set up and a K9 unit requested. Officer Gehrke and Police Dog Zach arrived on the scene with a 20-minute response time. It was broadcast by radio that the suspect was probably armed, although no weapon was seen.

Upon Gehrke's arrival, Sgt. Terry Oswald was contacted because he was the last person to see where the suspect went over the fence into the woods. Both Officer Gehrke and Sgt. Oswald went on the track after Zach was put over the 2 1/2 metre (eight-foot) high cyclone fence. Before Zach was put over the fence, he was air scenting so the officers knew the suspect was fairly close. As soon as Zach was put over the fence, he immediately picked up a track for about 45 metres (50 yards) along the fence and then tracked down into a very thick blackberry ravine where he engaged the suspect.

At this point, Zach was tracking off line and could not be seen; however, movement could be seen in the dense brush about 9 metres (30 feet) ahead. The officers heard five shots in rapid succession, fired by the suspect, and a muffled yelp on the third round fired. Officer Gehrke and Sgt. Oswald were only 6 metres (20 feet) from the scene and took cover by diving into the brush behind a large tree.

Gehrke tried to recall Zach once but he did not respond. Since they were only 8 metres (25 feet) from the suspect, only one recall was voiced, to prevent giving away their location. Realizing his dog was likley shot, Gehrke requested three additional K9 teams to respond. He wanted two handlers with a fresh dog to run with him and he wanted one team to prepare as a transport vehicle to take K9 Zach to Greenlake Clinic.

K9 Officers Bell and Klason arrived with Police Service Dog "Magnum" fifteen minutes later. Gehrke took them to where he had last seen Zach and K9 Magnum immediately began to air scent. He located the suspect lying down just ten feet on the other side of the brush pile. K9 Zach was lying next to the suspect and both the dog and the suspect had obvious head wounds.

Oswald and Gehrke carried out Zach to other K9 officers, who immediately initiated CPR. Dr. Canfield, the departmental veterinarian, gave instructions over the radio to a medic unit that arrived to assist. They tried to stabilize Zach for transportation to Greenlake Animal Hospital, but there was no heartbeat or respiration.

At the hospital Dr. Canfield followed necessary measures but pronounced Zach dead on arrival. Zach had been shot four times in the head with two bullets entering through the mouth. Dr. Canfield stated that any one of the head wounds was instantly fatal.

The suspect was taken to Harborview where he died a short time later of a bullet wound to the head, apparently self-inflicted.

Zach was awarded King County's Valor and Blue Star Awards for unselfishly giving his life in the line of duty for his fellow officers. He was born on December 9, 1982 and was sired by King County Police Dog Jake. Jake had been shot by a bank robber, once in the chest and once in the head with a .357 magnum, but survived his wounds to go on and live peaceably in retirement after six years of service.

K9 Liberty – Culver City, CA, 1989

A Culver City shooting occurred about 11 p.m, two hours after motorcycle officers from West Los Angeles chased two suspects in what turned out to be a stolen car. The pursuit ended at Washington Boulevard and Bledsoe Avenue in Culver City when the car crashed into a curb. After jumping out of the car, the driver fired at officers, missing them. When other officers arrived, a house by house search was conducted.

K9 Officer John Hall and his dog, Liberty, were searching a garage when they were hit by gunfire from a storage room. Hall was shot in the wrist. His partner Liberty, a female Rottweiler, was struck in the chest. Although wounded, Hall returned fire and took up another position near the front of the garage. The suspect emerged from the storage room and Hall fired several more shots from his 9-millimetre pistol, fatally wounding him.

A second K9 officer, Sgt. Mark Mooring, directed his German Shepherd, Friday, into the garage and found a second suspect. When the suspect pointed a handgun at Mooring, the officer fired his pistol three times, killing the offender. Hall was treated at hospital for gunshot wounds and a fractured arm. Liberty died at a local veterinary office.

K9 Billy – Sacramento, CA, 1989

A Sacramento Sheriff's Dept. Police Dog named "Billy" was killed August 6, 1989. Billy's handler, Deputy Keith Schmalz, saw a white Monte Carlo coming out from behind closed businesses in Sacramento, California. Schmalz followed the vehicle and saw the occupants throw something out of the window. The officer tried to stop the vehicle and a pursuit ensued. The pursuit ended at the rear of an apartment complex where two of the three occupants of the vehicle ran from officers.

The cover officer chased the passenger, and Officer Schmalz and K9 Billy went after the driver of the vehicle, chasing him into the apartment complex. As Officer Schmalz ran past the suspect vehicle he noted the third suspect slouched down in the back seat of the car. Officer Schmalz stopped to secure this suspect and K9 Billy continued to pursue the driver. After the third suspect was secured Officer Schmalz went to locate his dog.

About 68 metres (75 yards) away and deep into the apartment complex, he located his dog. Billy had been shot four times with a .22 calibre revolver and lay dying on the sidewalk. Officers rushed Billy to an emergency vet clinic where he was pronounced dead. Billy was a six-year-old German Shepherd that had worked for the department as a police dog for three years.

K9 Marko – Los Angeles, CA, 1989

K9 Marko was stabbed to death while pursuing a suspect for auto theft. The 27-year-old suspect stabbed Marko in the back of the head after the dog tracked him down and found him hiding beneath the front porch of a house.

Officer Apodaca found Marko lying in a pool of blood as fellow officers searched for the suspect. A special weapons team later used tear gas to flush the suspect out from under the house. The dog was airlifted by helicopter to an emergency animal hospital, however he died from his injuries.

Marko was a seven-year-old German Shepherd who had served the Los Angeles Police Dept since 1984. He was responsible for 243 felony arrests up to the time of his death.

K9 Lucky – Clarke County, WA, 1990

In May of 1990 Deputy Tom Mitchum and K9 Lucky responded to a shots fired call. A suspect had fled from a stolen vehicle and subsequently fired at pursuing officers. K9 Lucky was put on the track and tracked through the bush. As Lucky indicated they were getting close to the suspect he entered a heavy bush area and got out of sight of the handler. Moments later Deputy Mitchum and his backup officer heard a large calibre gunshot from the ridge above them. The officer felt that his dog was down and injured, if not killed. Darkness was nearing and more units closed in on the area. A plainclothes member doing containment reported via radio that he was holding a suspect at gunpoint. The suspect was in possession of a .357 magnum revolver and a .22 calibre semi auto handgun. The man admitted to shooting a dog and gave directions to where the dog could be located. Deputy Mitchum and assisting officers went back to the scene and found Lucky dead from a single gunshot wound to the chest. Autopsy reports indicate that K9 Lucky was in full charge when shot by the gunman.

Lucky was in service since 1987, credited in 1988 with 46 felony and 97 misdemeanor arrests. In 1989 he had 112 felony and 99 misdemeanor arrests. Prior to his death in 1990 he was responsible for 20 felony and 41 misdemeanor arrests in that year.

Deputy Tom Mitchum and K9 Lucky

K9 Kim – Huntington Beach, CA, 1991

On May 26, 1991 at 17:15 hours, Officer James Weaver stopped a vehicle for a routine traffic stop. As he approached the car, it suddenly sped away, starting a police pursuit. During the pursuit, the suspect vehicle got caught up in heavy traffic and the suspect bailed out of the car and fled on foot.

Officer Weaver released K9 Kim to track and the dog apprehended the suspect. The suspect produced a four-inch-long knife and repeatedly stabbed Kim. During the fight the dog held the suspect, resulting in the suspect receiving multiple wounds from the dog. However, in his panic the suspect stabbed himself in the leg during the confrontation.

Kim was airlifted to a veterinarian by helicopter. He was treated for multiple stab wounds, receiving blood transfusions and heart massage in attempts to save his life. He died three hours later.

Officer Jim Weaver and K9 Kim

K9 Star – Kansas City, MO, 1991

On November 18, 1991, Police K9 Star gave his life while searching a darkened house for a suspect wanted in the attempted murder of a police officer. K9 Star responded with other tactical officers when police had received a tip of the possible whereabouts of the suspect. Star's handler, Officer Patterson, gave a verbal warning that a dog was to be released to search the building. One subject came out, however it was not the suspect wanted by the police. Officer Patterson repeated the warning and receiving no response, released Star to search the building. The dog indicated a bedroom and entered the room. The dog located the suspect and barked, at which time two shots were fired. Officer Patterson recalled the dog, and Star managed to limp his way toward him, collapsing as he reached his handler. Officer Patterson picked up his partner and rushed him to the nearest veterinarian hospital, however Star was pronounced dead on arrival. Other officers at the scene pumped tear gas into the building, however it had no apparent effect on the suspect. He fired on the officers and was subsequently killed by return fire.

Star's real name was Koton. He starred in the movie "K9" with James Belushi. He was teamed with Officer Patterson for two years, and was responsible for over 24 felony arrests at the time of his death. Only ten days before he was killed, he was responsible for locating ten kilos of cocaine worth 1.2 million dollars. He was the fourth police dog to die in the line of duty in Kansas City.

K9 Training Log Entry (front)

K9 TRAINING LOG ENTRY

Training Location _____

Date ___ / ___ / ___
Shift Start _____ hrs
Shift End _____ hrs

TRAINING PROFILE

- ☐ Obedience
- ☐ Tracking
- ☐ Evidence Search
- ☐ Area Search
- ☐ Agility Course
- ☐ Criminal Apprehension
- ☐ Building Search
- ☐ Narcotics Detection
- ☐ Explosives Detection
- ☐ Tactical Exercise
- ☐ ERT/SWAT
- ☐ Other

Names Of Decoys/Agitators Used

1. _____ 2. _____

Details Of Exercise

_____
_____
_____
_____
_____
_____

Handler's Notes/Comments

_____
_____
_____
_____
_____
_____
_____
_____

Trainer's Comments

_____
_____
_____
_____

Trainer's Signature _____

©1993 K9 Academy For Law Enforcement / Eden & Ney Associates

K9 Training Log Entry (back)

Exercise Worksheet   Temperature:

[N]

When applicable, draw arrow in box to indicate wind direction. [ ]

Sketch of Terrain and Track Laid or Training Problem Layout

Tracking Applications
Tracking Legend: S - Indicates Starting Point of Track **X** - Indicates End of Track **A** - Indicates Article
Path Of Track Layer - - - -   Path Of K9 Team -------   Name of Tracklayer _____
Articles on Track _____
Distractions on Track _____

Terrain
❏ Pavement/Cement/Hard Surface   ❏ Grass   ❏ Bush/Heavy Forest   ❏ Sand/Gravel
❏ Industrial Area   ❏ Urban/Suburban Commercial   ❏ Urban/Suburban Residential   ❏ Rural

General Conditions
❏ Dry   ❏ Muggy   ❏ Wet   ❏ Light Rain   ❏ Med Rain
❏ Heavy Rain   ❏ Snow   ❏ Sunny   ❏ Cloudy   ❏ Overcast

Winds   Direction _____
❏ Still   ❏ Light   ❏ Medium   ❏ Strong

Temperatures
❏ Cold   ❏ Cool   ❏ Warm   ❏ Hot

Lighting Conditions
❏ Dark   ❏ Dawn   ❏ Daylight   ❏ Dusk

Time Records
Problem Set _____ hrs
K9 Started Exercise _____ hrs
Time Delay _____ minutes
Time Completed _____ hrs

K9 Handler's Signature

_____

©1993 K9 Academy For Law Enforcement / Eden & Ney Associates

K9 Usage Log (front)

K9 USAGE LOG

Case Number: _____   Date ___/___/___

K9 APPLICATION

- ❏ Public Demonstration
- ❏ Track
- ❏ Evidence Search
- ❏ Area Search

- ❏ Crowd Control
- ❏ Criminal Apprehension
- ❏ Building Search
- ❏ Narcotics Detection

- ❏ Explosives Detection
- ❏ ERT/SWAT
- ❏ Other

TIMES

Time Occurred _____ hrs
Time Requested _____ hrs
Time of Arrival _____ hrs
Time of Apprehension or Find _____ hrs

APPLICATION RESULTS

- ❏ Successful Application
- ❏ Unsuccessful Application
- ❏ Elimination Application
- ❏ Offence Unconfirmed

Summarized Details Of Event   ❏ **Bite Report**

_____
_____
_____

Handler's Notes

_____
_____
_____
_____
_____
_____
_____
_____
_____
_____
_____
_____
_____

©1993 K9 Academy For Law Enforcement / Eden & Ney Associates

K9 Usage Log (back)

Handler's Notes Cont.

_____
_____
_____
_____

[N]

When applicable, draw arrow in box to indicate wind direction. [ ]

Sketch of Terrain and Track or Search Area

Tracking Legend: **S** - Starting Point of Track **X** - Indicates End of Track **E** - Indicates Evidence
Path Of K9 Team ------ Evidence on Track _____
Officer(s) who retained recovered evidence: _____

Terrain
❑ Pavement/Cement/Hard Surface   ❑ Grass   ❑ Bush/Heavy Forest   ❑ Sand/Gravel
❑ Industrial Area   ❑ Commercial   ❑ Urban/Suburban Residential   ❑ Rural

General Conditions
❑ Dry   ❑ Muggy   ❑ Wet   ❑ Light Rain   ❑ Med Rain
❑ Heavy Rain   ❑ Snow   ❑ Sunny   ❑ Cloudy   ❑ Overcast

Winds Direction _____   ❑ Still   ❑ Light   ❑ Medium   ❑ Strong
Temperatures   ❑ Cold   ❑ Cool   ❑ Warm   ❑ Hot   Actual Temperature If Known _____
Lighting Conditions   ❑ Dark   ❑ Dawn   ❑ Daylight   ❑ Dusk

Suspect(s) Apprehended:
1._____
2._____

K9 Officer's Signature
_____

©1993 K9 Academy For Law Enforcement / Eden & Ney Associates